DEVOTIONAL FOR TEEN BOYS

LEVEL UP WITH EACH DEVOTION, BIBLE STUDY, AND PRAYER FOR UNSHAKABLE FAITH AND FEARLESS LEADERSHIP

HILLARY OLIVE

CONTENTS

I dedicate this book to my greatest blessings, my sons, Griffin and Maddox.

INTRODUCTION

Hey! Are you ready to take your relationship with God to the next level? My best guess would be since you are reading this, the answer to that question is probably, a yes. That's great! I'm so glad you are here! Getting to know God and actively seeking His face is never a bad idea. And, this book, along with your Bible, makes it easier than you might think. Fifteen to twenty minutes is all you need to read the chapter and answer the questions—questions that will make you think long and hard about who you are and how to become the guy God created you to be.

You also need to know that there is no set schedule you must stick to. Schedules are necessary for a lot of things, but this book isn't one of them. I would say, consistency is key. Afterall, you can't play sports, an instrument, or even video games without knowing the rules, goals and objectives, or without consistent practice. The same thing applies when developing a strong relationship with God. If there was a person you really wanted to get to know, wouldn't you want to spend quality time with them? You need to know what the Bible says. That's the only way you will know the kind of relationship God wants with you. Just like with any relationship, to feel like you are taking your relationship with God to the next level, you must put the effort in. But putting too much pressure on you to do that isn't what God wants, so there's no pressure here, either.

I understand I am not a male and I will not pretend to fully understand exactly what you are going through. Before creating this book, I interviewed incredible guys just like you all over the world. I asked about their strengths and weaknesses. I asked about their relationship with God through Jesus Christ and with their family and friends. I asked about their school life. Some of the guys I spoke with were homeschooled, others were freshmen in public school, I even spoke with guys who when to small private schools. I also spoke with a few graduates. I interviewed youth leaders and pastors and asked them what they saw their boys struggling with. I am pouring all of that into this book. A special thank you to all the young men involved.

With all that said, are you ready to grow into the confident, natural born leader God created you to be? Most importantly, are you ready to take your faith to the next level? Grab a notebook and let's get started.

1

THE LAYOUT OF THE PLAYING FIELD

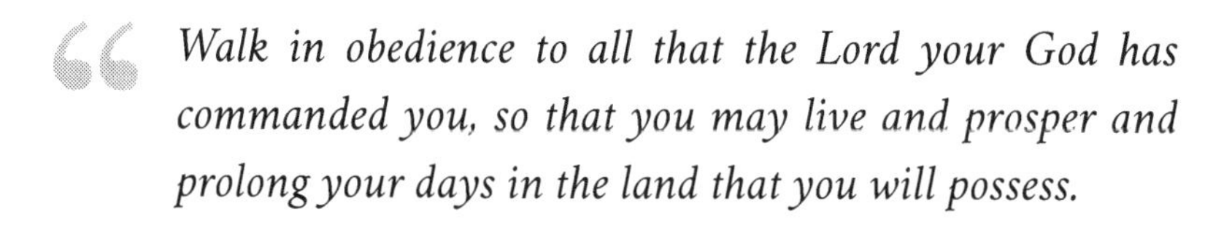

Walk in obedience to all that the Lord your God has commanded you, so that you may live and prosper and prolong your days in the land that you will possess.

— *DEUTERONOMY 5:33 NIV*

The devotions are short and to the point. Each one covers a topic that you need to deal with—hot topics that all guys your age face. Each devotion is also easy to follow. The format is the same for each chapter:

- Title
- Bible verse
- Real-life example
- Bible "Case in Point"
- Use it for YOU
- More Bible verses to look up

- A reminder to pray

The real-life example is your devotional portion of the chapter. Each one is a short, relatable story to encourage you to think about how the scripture applies to you in this season of your life. You will see real-life examples from my interviews as well as things you might have seen on TV or read about in a book. The Bible "Case in Point" is your Bible study portion. I strongly advise you to open your Bibles and read the summary in context. The "Case in Point" looks at a prime example or examples that backs up what is discussed in the devotional. References in this section will be from the New International Version (NIV), but you can use any Bible version you have. Some of the verses might be off by a number or two. The "Use it for YOU" section is the play that brings it all home. These are your reflection questions and opportunity to dive deep inwards. If you take these seriously, expect massive growth. If any question is too big or not relevant, pray over it and move on. Exactly as it says, use it for YOU. This is followed by more verses to look up that is relevant to the topic, and lastly the chapter ends with a prayer prompt. You may want to grab a blank notebook to write down any notes and thoughts from the Bible study along with your answers to the reflections.

See? It's simple but full of important stuff that will make your life better, safer, and way more exciting and rewarding than you could ever achieve on your own.

2

IT ALL STARTS WITH PRAYER

> *Do not be anxious about anything, but in every situation, by prayer and petition, with thanksgiving, present your requests to God. And the peace of God, which transcends all understanding, will guard your hearts and your minds in Christ Jesus.*
>
> — *PHILIPPIANS 4:6–7 NIV*

Prayer is the way we talk to God. And since this book is all about getting to know God better, talking to Him is number one on the to-do list. You can't know God unless you talk to Him and let Him talk to you. Talking and listening are the basic building blocks for healthy communication with anyone including God. Communication in life is key to any relationship!

Think about it: on the basketball court, on the soccer field, in the classroom, at home, driving down the street…it doesn't matter where you go or who you are with, you have to communicate. Otherwise, you wouldn't be an actual team. If there is no communication in the classroom you wouldn't learn enough to understand your homework assignments, also you and your parents' relationship will be…well, we won't even go there! And driving without communication, well, that would be like a real live pinball machine.

When it comes to your relationship with God, communication is key. Without talking to God, and letting Him talk to you, it isn't possible to know Him, know what He expects from you, and what He wants for your life. So, pray. Pray about everything. Don't hold back. God knows what's on your mind, anyway, but He still likes to hear you say it. Don't hold back. Talk to Him like He's your best friend. Be honest. Nothing shocks Him. There's nothing He can't handle when you put your faith in Him.

CASE IN POINT

In Psalm 5:3 (NIV), David tells us that the first thing he does every morning is talk to God. David prays and then he waits *expectantly* for God to answer him, because he knows He will. In Psalm 43, David asks God why God has rejected him. He doubted God's protection and love. But only for a little while, because the more David prays, the more he realized God was there and that he was wrong for doubting God.

See? Everyone struggles with talking and listening to God. Another thing people struggle with is believing God answers our prayers, but He does. Every single one of them. Sometimes the answer is no. Sometimes the answer is yes. Sometimes the answer is not yet. But there is always an answer. Wait a minute! What about those verses that say we can ask for whatever we want, and God will give it to us?

Actually, it says whatever we ask for *in Jesus' name.* It also either comes before or after verses that talk about wanting only what will bring us closer to God. So, if you are asking for things that will be more important to you than your relationship with God or will cause you to do something that is sinful or will dishonor God, then the answer will be no. It's not all that different from asking your parents for something that they know isn't right or good for you.

USE IT FOR YOU

1. How often do you talk to God? Do you spend time every day telling God thank you for all the blessings in your life? Do you pray for other people? When you are in a tough situation do you ask God for guidance? Ask God to show and tell you what He wants you to do. Tell Him what you need and want.

2. How has God answered your prayers? When has He told you yes, no, and not yet?

3. What changes do you need to make in your schedule to make more time for prayer? How will you make those changes to communicate more with God?

4. I challenge you to start a journal of prayers to God and make a note of how He answered your prayers.

5. Do you ever wonder how your parents talk to God? Let's ask them. What did they say?

MORE FROM THE BIBLE

Look up the following verses. Read each one and think about what it is saying to YOU.

- Matthew 6:5–13
- Matthew 26:41
- James 4:3
- John 14:13

PRAYER PROMPT

Read Matthew 6:5–13 again and spend a few minutes praying the way Jesus instructed us to pray.

3

FROM THE INSIDE OUT

> *But the Lord said to Samuel, "Do not consider his appearance or his height, for I have rejected him. The Lord does not look at the things people look at. People look at the outward appearance, but the Lord looks at the heart."*
>
> — *1 SAMUEL 16:7 NIV*

Aaron Hernandez, Edawn Coughman, and Ray Rice. Do you know who they are? All three are former NFL players. From the outside, all three looked like they were living the dream. They seemed to have everything a guy could want—a successful career, lots of money, popularity, fancy cars, houses, and whatever else they wanted. Yep, they looked pretty good... from the outside.

But on the inside things were different...and ugly. Hernandez murdered someone and was sentenced to life in prison. Coughman destroyed his own property to fake a hate crime he said was done because he was black. Rice severely abused his fiancée and was blacklisted from ever playing pro football again.

When it comes to your identity, what you look like, how much money you have, or even how smart or athletic you are, the outside is not what matters. What matters is who you are from the inside out. If you think that sounds cheesy, think about why your friends are your friends. Is it because you made varsity as a freshman or because they can trust you and treat you like friends should? Do you have more respect for a coach who respects you and your teammates or one who puts on a show for parents but when it's just him and you, he treats you like dirt? Would you rather have a math teacher who takes the time to explain things, or one that acts like anyone who isn't a math whiz is doomed for failure?

CASE IN POINT

The Pharisees, leaders of the Jewish people and the temple, were all about appearances, popularity, and being in charge. They never missed a chance to let people know how important they were. Jesus saw right through them, though, and let's just say He wasn't impressed. In fact, Jesus never missed a chance to let them know that God wasn't impressed with them, either.

In Matthew 23:25–26, Jesus literally tells them to clean up their act. Instead of telling you what He said, take a minute to read it for yourself. It's powerful.

> *"Woe to you, teachers of the law and Pharisees, you hypocrites! You clean the outside of the cup and dish, but inside they are full of greed and self-indulgence. Blind Pharisee! First clean the inside of the cup and dish, and then the outside also will be clean."*
>
> — *(NIV)*

Blunt? Yes. But when it comes to a relationship with God, nobody (especially God) wants to mess with someone pretending to be who and what they aren't. God *does* expect you to take care of your body by using good hygiene, eating a healthy diet, exercising, and not abusing it in any way, but the brand of shoes or clothes you wear, or whether you have zits or not isn't what matters to God. It is your character and personality—those things that work their way out from inside of you —that matter most to God, and anyone else worth hanging out with, too.

USE IT FOR YOU

1. Write down the names of your three best friends and why they are your friends.

2. What five qualities about yourself do you want people to notice and appreciate most?

3. Have you ever chosen a friend based on what they looked like or their status? How did that work out for you? Has someone done that to you?

4. Do you think society puts too much pressure on guys (and girls) to look and act a certain way? If so, what can YOU do to change that—even if the only person you change is yourself?

5. If there a friend in your life going through a tough time; or is there someone that you care about but have not spoken to in a while? I challenge you to pray for them and then to pick up the phone give them a call or text. Let them know you care and that you are thinking of them.

MORE FROM THE BIBLE

Look up the following verses. Read each one and think about what it is saying to YOU.

- Genesis 1:27
- Psalm 139:1–18

PRAYER PROMPT

Pray for confidence to be yourself. Pray for good, solid friendships. People that will show up for you. Pray for God to give you opportunities to use your talents and abilities in ways that will honor God and make Him proud of you.

4

EVERYONE HAS VALUE

> *So, in everything, do to others what you would have them do to you, for this sums up the Law and the Prophets.*
>
> — *MATTHEW 7:12 NIV*

Zach was one of the best of the best cross country and distance runner in track when he was in junior high and high school. He qualified for state all four years and medaled two of them. That would have been enough to gain the attention and respect of his coaches and teammates, but that wasn't what stood out to them. It was Zach's willingness to see and recognize the value of every other member of his team, including Arley.

Arley was the guy who ran for all he was worth but always came in last...or nearly so. Arley was the guy who was so shy most people never even noticed him. He was the guy who always sat alone in the lunchroom. Arley was the last guy you would have thought Zach would have 'bothered' with, but Zach didn't see Arley as a "bother". To Zach, Arley was just a guy who needed to know his efforts mattered. To Zach, Arley was a guy who deserved to be treated like the athlete that he was—a runner who showed up and finished the race no matter what. To Zach, Arley was a guy who had feelings like everyone else, and who deserved to know that he had a friend in Zach.

CASE IN POINT

You have probably heard of Paul, one of the first missionaries ever. He is also the guy who wrote almost half the books in the New Testament—thirteen in all. He gave 100% '+' to teaching people to know and love God and accept Jesus as their Savior. But Paul wasn't always all-in for Jesus. He was a totally different kind of guy before he became a missionary. He even had a different name—Saul.

Saul hated Christians. He beat them, put them in jail, and watched while even worse things happened to them. But God's plan for Saul was much grander that Saul could have possible imagined. God knew that a guy with that much energy and passion for whatever he did, was just what He needed to teach people the truth about Jesus and how to be a Christian. There was just one little problem...

Back when Paul was still Saul in Acts 9, he was in on trying to arrest and abuse Jesus' disciples after He went back to heaven. So, when Paul showed up and said he has changed and wanted to be one of them, they didn't believe it. Everyone thought it was a trick. Everyone except a guy named Barnabas. Barnabas wasn't one of Jesus' twelve disciples, but he was a close follower of Jesus. He was an active and dedicated worker in getting the first Church started, and the disciples trusted him. So, after Barnabas told them about Paul and how God changed his life while he was on his way to Damascus to put more Christians in prison nonetheless, they welcomed Paul into the family of God.

The takeaway from all of this is that Barnabas took the time to see Paul for who he was after he accepted Jesus as his Savior, even when others wouldn't. Barnabas remembered something we all need to remember—that God values everyone, so we should, too. One more key takeaway from this is that it does not matter how dark your past is, or all the things you've done wrong, or how broken you may feel. God can still use you. He has a plan for you. He is not mad at you, He loves you. If what you are going through is not good; that means He is not done refining you.

USE IT FOR YOU

1. Who are the "Arleys" in your school, in your neighborhood, or on your team? How do you treat them?

2. Have you ever ignored someone, stopped talking to someone, or bullied someone because other kids were doing so? Why did you do it? How did it make you feel?

3. Have you ever felt like you are an "Arley"? If so, when and why?

4. Will you step up and be a Barnabas to the "Arleys" you know? If so, how? If not, why not?

5. If you are "Arley," who can be your Barnabas? Ask God to make it happen for you.

MORE FROM THE BIBLE

Look up the following verses. Read each one and think about what it is saying to YOU.

- 1 Corinthians 12:14–18
- Proverbs 17:17
- 1 Corinthians 10:24

PRAYER PROMPT

Pray for courage to reach out to the "Arleys" in your school.

Pray for confidence to always do your best and be your best self…and know that you are enough.

5

IDENTITY: EYES ON YOU

> *You are the light of the world. A city on a hill cannot be hidden. Neither do people light a lamp and put it under a bowl. Instead, they put it on its stand, and it gives light to everyone in the house. In the same way, let your light shine before men, that they may see your good deeds and praise your Father in heaven.*
>
> — *MATTHEW 5:14–16 NIV*

Back in 2006, before you were even born, country music star, Rodney Atkins released a song called, "Watching You." The song talks about how kids watch and mimic their parents.

We see that after the Tokyo Summer Olympics in 2021; the number of kids who started taking gymnastics lessons increased by over 10%. Hockey and swimming lessons also grew by at least that much. Why? Because kids and teenagers, maybe even you, were watching the athletes and decided they wanted to be like them.

Here's the thing, though, you don't have to be famous to be watched. If you stop and think about it, there are probably two or three people *you* look up to. Who are they? Are they famous or are they *just* people you know? People who you invest interest in can be a mentor, teacher, coach, parent, grandparent, or even a friend.

Something else you need to know is that YOU are also being looked up to and probably watched by someone. Maybe even several people. They may be watching you because they want to be like you. They may be watching you to see if your actions match your words, i.e., are you who you claim to be? Either way, they are watching you, so you need to make sure you are leaving the impression you want to leave on others, the same impression you would want your mentor or friend to leave on you.

CASE IN POINT

Let's talk about Daniel. Daniel was most likely a teenager like you when the Babylonians beat down the Israelites and took over their entire country. They took most of the people from Israel to Babylon, which was in what we now know as Iraq.

You see in Daniel 6:10 that Daniel was totally committed to God. He wouldn't budge when it came to doing what pleased and honored God. From the food he ate (and wouldn't eat) to refusing to pray to anyone but God, Daniel stood his ground.

King Darius admired Daniel's integrity, faith, and loyalty to God so much that he appointed Daniel as one of the official administrators over the kingdom. There were some serious jealousy issues with some other guys in the court. They watched Daniel like a hawk, trying to find a way to get him in trouble and thrown out. These bad guys devised a plan that would eventually trick the king into signing a decree that said no one could pray to anyone but the king for thirty days. Daniel refused to pray to anyone but God and ended up being thrown into a pit of lions. BUT...

Because Daniel didn't back down from his faith, God protected Daniel. The lions didn't even touch him—not even a nibble! So, make sure that the people who are watching you (because they are), see the guy God wants and needs you to be.

USE IT FOR YOU

1. Who do you look up to and why?

Bonus challenge: Tell your person that you look up to them and why.

2. Who do you think might be watching you?

3, What would they see? Are you setting the right example?

4. If you are a Christian, would it be a surprise for people to know that about you? Why or why not?

5: List three things about yourself you want to improve, to set a good example to the people who are watching you.

MORE FROM THE BIBLE

Look up the following verses. Read each one and think about what it is saying to YOU.

- Daniel chapter 1
- 1 Timothy 4:12
- Hebrews 13:7

PRAYER PROMPT

Pray that you will be proud to let people know you are a Christian.

Pray that God will help you say the right thing, do the right thing, and choose friends who don't try to pull you away from God.

6

IT'S NOT ALL ABOUT YOU

> *I have been crucified with Christ and I no longer live, but Christ lives in me. The life I live in the body, I live by faith in the Son of God who loved me and gave Himself for me.*
>
> — *GALATIANS 2:20 NIV*

If you don't already have your driver's license, there's a good chance you are already counting down the days, months, or maybe even the years before you do. Getting that little piece of plastic is a *big* deal. You need to understand, though, that the little piece of plastic and the power that comes with it is not something you have a right to. It is a privilege you earn...and one that comes with a massive amount of responsibility.

A driver's license comes with the responsibility to follow the rules of the road and to be a responsible and cautious driver.

Getting a driver's license—the one you studied and practiced so hard to get—doesn't mean you can toss all that stuff you learned out the window. The speed limits, road signs, and all the other driving rules still count. You still must obey them, or you will pay the consequences. You also need to remember that not only are you responsible for your life and your vehicle, but you have a certain amount of responsibility for the other people driving around you, too.

Now, let's look at what this means to you and your relationship with God. When you accept Jesus as your Lord and Savior, you are *promising* to obey God's commands and expectations that are in the Bible. You are *promising* to represent God's family in a way that will make Him proud and that might cause someone else to want to be part of God's family, too. So, while getting a driver's license *is* a big deal, being saved through Jesus is even bigger. Salvation is a gift. A free gift. But it is also a gift that comes with the responsibility of using it wisely and rightly.

CASE IN POINT

In the Old Testament book of 2 Samuel: 24, King David ignored his responsibility to trust God completely. He disobeyed God outright by counting the number of men in his army. You might not think that's a big deal—that it's actually a good idea to know how many men you've got. But God had instructed David specifically not to do that—to trust Him that the army would always be ready to fight and win, no matter the size of his army or the size of the enemy's army.

As soon as David got the results of the count, he was sorry and ashamed for what he'd done. God had to discipline him, though, so He did. It was not a pretty sight, but you can read that for yourself later. What you need to know now is that David admitted he had sinned. He asked God to forgive him, and then promised God that he would never disobey Him again. David kept that promise. He didn't just say it, David made a sacrifice to God (they did that a lot back then).

When he got to the place where he was going to make the sacrifice, the man who owned the land told King David it would be an honor to give him the land. David refused to take it without paying for it. He said, "I will not offer to the LORD sacrifices which cost me nothing." In other words, even King David understood that he was God's child and that he had a responsibility to honor God in everything he said and did. No shortcuts. He knew God was all-in with him, so he was all-in with God.

USE IT FOR YOU:

1: Be honest—do you believe everything the Bible says is true? Why or why not? After you answer, find 2 Timothy 3:16–17 and read it.

2: Do these verses change your answer to question 1?

3: What do you think is the hardest part about being a Christian and why?

4: What can you do to try to help you deal with these things mentioned previously?

5. Are you battling with anything right now? Mentally, Physically, Emotionally? Does the enemy seem large and scary? Is there something that you need to fully let go and surrender to God? Always remember, you are never alone, and you are never abandoned.

MORE FROM THE BIBLE

Look up the following verses. Read each one and think about what it is saying to YOU.

- 2 Samuel 24:24
- Ephesians 5:1

PRAYER PROMPT

Be honest with God. Tell Him what you don't understand and ask Him to help you find clarity. Tell God what makes it hard for you to obey Him and ask Him to help you do better. Pray to God to calm any storms that you may be facing and to help you defeat any enemy that could be weighing on you.

7

YOUR LIFE IS AN OCCASION...RISE TO IT!

> *So, whether you eat or drink or whatever you do, do it all for the glory of God.*
>
> — 1ST CORINTHIANS 10:31 NIV

The title to this chapter is a quote from the movie, *Mr. Magorium's Wonder Emporium.* It's probably not one you've seen, because it didn't get the best reviews. The storyline is for little kids, but most of the characters are grownups, so it doesn't really "fit" anywhere. But there are some really great things about the movie, and one of them is the friendship between two of the leading characters—Mr. Magorium and Molly Mahoney.

Molly, who is in her twenties, has worked for Mr. Magorium since she was a kid. She never left because she was too afraid to go after her dreams of being a concert pianist because...because she thought she might not make it. She thought she might fail. Mr. Magorium knew better. He knew Molly could do and be whatever she wanted, and he did everything he could to help her see that.

Your life is an occasion too. Do you know what that means? It means your life is full of opportunities, possibilities, and hope. When God created you, He gave you *everything* you need to be strong, courageous, and successful. Successful at what, you ask? Successful at *whatever* God gives you to do.

The world's version of success might come your way, too, but it won't fill that space we all have inside that makes us feel complete. The only way to do that is to make God your number one priority and make sure your life doesn't embarrass or disappoint God. It's like disappointing your parents and giving your family a "bad name," but multiplied by a zillion, at least.

CASE IN POINT

Looking at Genesis 37:3–4, Joseph was his dad's favorite son. I know—not cool to have a favorite, but he did. Some would say they think Joseph let this go to his head and that bragging about it made his older brothers hate Joseph. Hate—that's a strong word, but that's what it was. Anyway, there are two reasons I don't think Joseph was that kind of guy. Reason number one: he never does anything else to give us that impression. And if you know anything about Joseph, you know he had plenty of opportunities to brag and boast. Reason number two: God doesn't choose people who are full of themselves to do the type of things He did through Joseph. Joseph was humble, patient, and a walking, talking example of what forgiveness and mercy are all about.

USE IT FOR YOU

1. Take some time to think about what it is you really want out of life. What do you want to do career-wise? Where do you want to live? Do you want to get married and have kids…someday?

2: Where does God fit into your answers to question number one?

3: What would God have to say about the way you spent the last three days?

4: What changes need to be made so that your answer to question number three will be in line with the verse at the beginning of this chapter, *"So whether you eat or drink or whatever you do, do it all for the glory of God." ~1 Corinthians 10:31 NIV*

MORE FROM THE BIBLE

Look up the following verses. Read each one and think about what it is saying to YOU.

- Hebrews 13:7
- Titus 2:12
- Philippians 4:13

PRAYER PROMPT

Pray for faith that God knows what is best for your life—today and in the future.

Ask God to lead you, then listen and obey Him.

8

A BRIGHT FUTURE

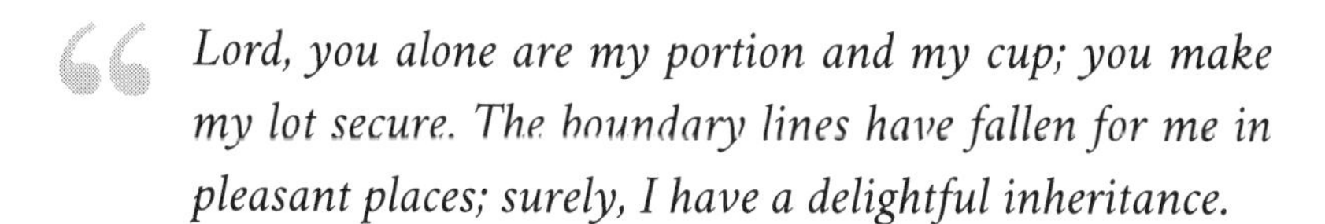

> *Lord, you alone are my portion and my cup; you make my lot secure. The boundary lines have fallen for me in pleasant places; surely, I have a delightful inheritance.*
>
> — *PSALM 16:5–6 NIV*

The Psalms by David have a lot of fancy words—words you would never use. You might not even know what some of them mean. Don't worry, though, that's about to change.

Portion and cup are another way to say, you are all I need to be content and satisfied from the inside out. A **secure lot** is a safety net—a fence or boundary line God can and will put around you that protects you from things that can hurt you—including yourself. David's comment about **pleasant places** is his way of saying thank you to God. He realized that God knows what's best for him and that doing life on God's terms is the surest way...the *only* way. David's closing comment about the **delightful inheritance** might sound like something your grandma would say, but that doesn't mean it's only for older people. A delightful inheritance is what God gives you—what He gives everyone—who lives within the boundaries He puts around you. That inheritance...it's called Heaven.

CASE IN POINT

God told Abraham in Genesis 12:1–3 to leave his homeland and go somewhere else, Abraham did it without question. When he got there, God told Abraham to look around, because as far as Abraham could see (and beyond) would be "home" to Abraham's descendants forever. This is a great example of physical boundaries.

Shadrach, Meshach, and Abednego from chapter three of the book of Daniel were three Jewish captives who refused to worship a false golden idol made king Nebuchadnezzar. They had strong moral boundaries and no matter what threat the king through their way they held firm and God saw this and kept them safe.

USE IT FOR YOU

1. What boundaries have your parents placed around you?

2. Do you feel these boundaries are fair? Why or why not? Do you understand why they are there? Why or why not?

3. If you were sitting across the table from God, what would you ask Him to do for you? What would you tell Him you want out of life?

4. If God were to reveal to you that He has an even better plan for your life than what you have requested, but chooses not to tell you the details, how would you respond?

MORE FROM THE BIBLE

Look up the following verses. Read each one and think about what it is saying to YOU.

- Isaiah 26:3
- Philippians 4:19
- 2 Corinthians 5:7

PRAYER PROMPT

Spill your guts to God. Tell Him what you want and what you need. Confess your sins and ask for forgiveness. Tell Him what scares you, what makes you angry, and ask for help handling these things. Ask God to help you make good choices and be respectful, kind, and obedient.

9

STRESS AND FAITH ARE LIKE OIL AND WATER—THEY DON'T MIX

> *Out of my distress I called on the Lord; the Lord answered me and set me free. The Lord is on my side; I will not fear. What can man do to me?*
>
> — *PSALM 118:5–6*

I asked youth pastor Dusty to pick one thing that he saw his kids struggle with the most, and I was not surprised when he said, it was stress and how to manage it. The demands on teenagers to get the best grades, have the most followers, pitch a no hitter, and spend quality time with family, and have college applications filled out yesterday; makes you feel exhausted just reading this sentence.

Everyone knows stress is bad for you. It causes all sorts of physical problems in your body. It can damage your heart. It can cause you to not be able to eat or digest your food or maybe even cause you to eat too much. Stress is also bad for your mental and emotional health. Depression, anxiety, eating disorders, drugs and alcohol abuse, thoughts about suicide...all these things can happen when you let stress take over you. There's nothing good on that list of things stress can do to a person, so why do you let stress get to you? Why does anyone? Does stressing over a test get you a better grade? Does stressing about the argument you had with your parents make things better?

So, take it from Bob, Larry, and the Bible—stress isn't the way to deal with your problems or handle your anger and frustrations. Stress won't make the things you are afraid of any less scary. Only God can help with those things.

Here's a three-step solution to stress management:

1. Our performance driven society encourages you to be on go mode for every waking hour. This mindset will always leave you feeling burnt out. You need to schedule yourself time to *rest*. Rest your mind and body. Read Mathew 11:28-29
2. It is ok to be a *follower*. When you are in a relationship with Jesus, you can let your stress melt away knowing that the ultimate leader has the absolute best life planned for you already. Following Jesus does not equal weakness; it equals trust. Read John 8:12
3. There is power in *surrender*. Relinquish control over the stresses you are carrying and give your burdens to God; allow His presence to fill you up. Gods got this. Read John 14:3

CASE IN POINT

In 1 Samuel 18, King Saul (not the same Saul who changed his name to Paul) let jealousy stress him out so much that he tried to kill David (King David). Not just once. Not twice. Not even three times. He was on a mission and didn't intend to stop until he got the job done. Do you know what happened? The stress from all that anger and hate ended up getting King Saul killed.

The disciple Peter had a lot of stress to deal with, too. Can you imagine how you would feel if you out and out lied about knowing Jesus *three* times? You heard right – *three* times! But instead of letting the guilt and stress ruin his life and his relationship with Jesus, he gave it to God. He asked for forgiveness and embraced it. Peter exchanged the stress of feeling guilty for the peace of knowing that God didn't hold any of that against him. You can read more about Peter in Matthew 26:69–75, Mark 14:66–72, Luke 22:54–62, and John 18:15–27.

USE IT FOR YOU

1.What stresses you out right now?

2. How do you deal with your stress? What do you do to get rid of it?

3. How often do you ask God to help you instead of trying to do it all on your own?

4. The next time a stressful situation comes up or for the next finals week remember the three steps: rest, follow, surrender. Make a plan. When things start to get tense, you know what to do.

MORE FROM THE BIBLE

Look up the following verses. Read each one and think about what it is saying to YOU.

- Matthew 6:34
- Romans 8:31
- Psalm 94:19

PRAYER PROMPT

Take a few minutes right now to ask God to take away any stress you have and replace it with faith and courage to deal with it *with* God.

10

IT'S OKAY TO GET MAD...JUST DON'T GET EVEN

In your anger do not sin. Do not let the sun go down while you are still angry

— *EPHESIANS 4:26 NIV*

Do you see what that verse says? What it really says? It says *in* your anger, do not sin. That means don't sin when you are angry. It says nothing about anger *being* a sin. I don't know about you, but I'm relieved to know it's okay to get mad as long as we don't let it get the best of us. But you can't just use this as a permission slip to get mad. You need to remember that you can't let anger cause you to sin.

Getting even with someone who hurts you or makes you mad... that's a sin. Even if they started it. Breaking something, calling people names, disrespecting someone's property, cheating, lying, disobeying your parents, teachers, or anyone who has authority over you when you are mad...that's a sin. No excuses. None. Zero.

CASE IN POINT

The Bible tells us that Moses was humble—humbler than anyone else. Ever. That's amazing when you think about all the things God gave Moses the power to do. He parted the Red Sea. He stood up to Pharaoh a bunch of times. He led hundreds of thousands of Israelites around in the desert for forty years. He even talked to God face to face! And, of course, he took the Ten Commandments, and the rest of the Law after God wrote it on stones and read it to the Israelites. BUT...

Moses got angry. A lot. The Israelites gave him all sorts of reasons to get angry. They were ungrateful, disrespectful, impatient, and just downright hateful. One time, Moses got so mad he threw the stone tablets God had written on and broke them. God understood, though, and wrote them a second time. The only time God didn't excuse Moses' anger was the time his anger caused him to disobey God.

In Numbers 20:7–12, Moses was so mad that he ignored God's instructions on how to get the Israelites safe drinking water. God couldn't let that one slide, so he punished Moses. Big time. If you want to know more about what happened, read Numbers 20:2–13. But, for now, what you need to remember is that sinning because you are angry is no different from sinning because you think it will be fun. Or cool. Or harmless. God disciplines us every time we sin. Sometimes, like with Moses, He punishes us. So, remember that it's okay to get angry. Anger is a natural and temporary emotion. It is what we do with that anger that could leave a harsh impact on ourselves or others around us. Diffuse your anger wisely.

USE IT FOR YOU

1. What has made you angry recently?

2. What do you usually do when you get angry? How do you calm down?

3. Have you ever hurt someone or something, like punch a wall, because you were angry? How did that make you feel afterwards?

4. Has someone ever hurt you because they were angry? How did you deal with this situation?

5. Make a list of things you can do when you are angry to help you calm down without sinning and hurting others.

MORE FROM THE BIBLE

Look up the following verses. Read each one and think about what it is saying to YOU.

- Proverbs 19:11
- Ecclesiastes 7:9
- Proverbs 16:32

PRAYER PROMPT

Pray that God will help you control your temper, that you will not expect everything to go your way, and that you will learn to think before you speak.

11

THE WHOLE TRUTH AND NOTHING BUT THE TRUTH

> *Let your speech always be gracious, seasoned with salt, so that you may know how you ought to answer each person.*
>
> — COLOSSIANS 4:6 ESV

Timothy had a big presentation coming up at school. He planned to compare the impact of the Industrial Revolution on the way people worked and lived to today's booming technological growth in front of the entire seventh grade. Tim wanted to do his absolute best with this project but knew his public speaking skills needed improving. A good leader knows his strengths and weaknesses and when to ask for outside help. Tim met Dorian at his connect group at church. He was a grade ahead of him and remembered how brilliant Dorian's presentation was last year. Not only was Dorian a real history buff, but he also took a public speaking class and said he'd be happy to help. Dorian taught Tim how to do proper research, but most importantly, he also taught him how to present it in a compelling and easy-to-understand way.

The day of the presentation finally arrived, and Timothy blew the whole project out of the water! His teachers and principal praised him for his explicit knowledge of the subject and the way he presented. "We cannot believe you did this all by yourself! Well done!" Tim soaked up the praise and even won first place. However, not once did he mention Dorian.

That night at the dinner table, while his family was continuing the praise, Tim could not eat. He stayed awake all night, knowing he could not have done what he did today without Dorian's help, and the whole thing felt half a lie.

> *"A good leader takes a little more than his share of the blame, a little less than his share of the credit."*
>
> — *ARNOLD GLASOW, HUMORIST AND AUTHOR*

Tim knew what he had to do. The next day, Tim marched straight into the principal's office and told him the truth about not doing the whole project himself. He explained all the valuable lessons he had learned from Dorian and that he could not take all the credit. The principal was so impressed with Tim's story and told him that the most valuable lesson was learned just then. Tim got to keep his first-place position, and a new program at his school for mentorship was founded.

What about you? Have you ever spewed out words without thinking about how they would sound or how they would make someone feel? I think everyone has. What about all those times you've talked back to your parents? Lied about something, which led to another lie and another and another and....? Or maybe you exaggerated (stretch the truth) about your grades, your skills on the football field, the size of the buck you shot last deer season, or about you and your girlfriend. What happened when you did this—when your words weren't the truth, the whole truth and nothing but the truth? Did you feel a guilty weight on your back? Did you feel paranoid about getting caught?

Truth is a big deal. A *really* big deal. When you tell the truth you don't have to try to keep your lies and stories straight. You don't have to worry about getting caught. Telling the truth is a surefire way to have a better relationship with your parents, teachers, and friends. Telling the truth keeps you out of trouble, you'll do better in school, and you will feel more confident in your decisions and in the way speak to people. Drop the heavy weights and stand up taller. The truth and God's Truth are the only way.

CASE IN POINT

In Genesis, Jacob is the best-worst example of what happens when you don't tell the whole truth and nothing but the truth. Every. Single. Time. You. Open. Your. Mouth. Without going into detail, let's do a quick recap of Jacob's life of lies...

- Jacob lied to his dad who was old, blind, and dying. Jacob and his mom plotted out every little detail on how to lie to Isaac so that Jacob would get the inheritance his older brother, Esau, was supposed to get.
- Jacob lied and schemed against his father-in-law, whose name was Laban, more than once. One of the biggest lies Jacob told was when he tricked Laban out of the best sheep so Jacob could have more money.

Jacob the liar was lied to, too. His father in-law lied to him. His wives lied to him. His sons lied to him. As you can figure out, all these lies made their lives messy. BUT...

God still used Jacob in a big way. When Jacob finally decided to straighten up and be the man God created him to be, He used Jacob and his twelve sons to be the first generation of the entire Israelite nation. That means the moral of this true story is this: God expects and wants you to tell the truth, and when you do, you can be sure He lets you know how glad and proud He is of you because of it.

USE IT FOR YOU

1: What have you lied about? Why did you tell the lies you told?

2: Did you get caught? If so, what happened? If not, how does it feel having to always be on guard to cover your tracks?

3: How do you feel when you find out someone has lied to you? How does it change what you think about that person?

4: If you have any lies hanging out there, ones that haven't been uncovered, confess them to God (even though He already knows), and ask Him for the courage to go to the person, or people, you lied to and tell the truth. It won't be easy, and you might have some consequences to pay because of it. No matter what those consequences are, it will be better than living with the lie.

MORE FROM THE BIBLE

Look up the following verses. Read each one and think about what it is saying to YOU.

- Zechariah 8:16
- Proverbs 28:13
- Psalm 34:13

PRAYER PROMPT

Ask God to forgive you for the lies you have told and for the courage to always tell the truth.

12

GUARD YOUR WORDS

Set a guard, O Lord, over my mouth; keep watch over the door of my lips!

— *PSALM 141:3 ESV*

Jeremy and his best buddies loved to play video games. After a long day of school, soccer and homework he enjoyed playing a couple rounds of *Call of Duty* before going to bed. They had a whole squad every night. Jeremy was not the best player, and the other boys were not so kind about letting him know. The guys would say the meanest, foulest, things to Jeremy through the headset. The boys would never say those things to Jeremy's face and most of the time didn't even mean it. They were just joking they said. Eventually, Jeremy could not help but feel so low, depressed, even dreaded the game, but feared what the boys would think if he stopped playing. They were just joking right? Wrong. Whoever invented that terrible rhyme about sticks and stones was dead wrong. Words cut deep and create unseen wounds that will never fully heal without making a true amends. Jeremy finally revealed to his best friends about how he truly felt. The boys had no idea how much it affected him and their friendship.

CASE IN POINT

When Jesus gave His famous sermon on the Mount, He knew the weight that our words could have on one another. He also made it extremely clear that we must be held accountable for the words that we speak. According to Mathew 12:36 (KJV) Jesus said, "I say to you that for every idle word men may speak, they will give account for it in the day of judgement."

The word "idle" comes from the Greek word "argos," which can be translated as "inactive," "useless," or "unproductive." Jesus is saying that we will be held accountable for every word we speak that is frivolous, unproductive, or lacking in purpose. The ESV says "for every careless word" and the NIV says "for every empty word" that we speak. This includes gossip, slander, and any speech that does not contribute to building up others or honoring God. Jesus is emphasizing the importance of using our words wisely and for good. Notice how Jesus gives a strong reminder about judgement day right after He talks about choosing our words wisely. Therefore, it is important to use our words carefully and to strive to speak only that which is true, kind, and beneficial.

USE IT FOR YOU

1: Who or what makes it hard for you to guard your words?

2: Would you say you are easygoing? Or are you hot-tempered?

3: When have you said something you shouldn't? What happened? Did you try to make things right afterwards?

4: How did you handle it when people said things to you that they shouldn't have done so?

MORE FROM THE BIBLE

Look up the following verses. Read each one and think about what it is saying to YOU.

- James 1:19
- Ephesians 4:29
- Proverbs 14:25

PRAYER PROMPT

Pray that God will help you know when to speak up, and to give you the right words to say.

Pray that God will help you use your words wisely and to help people instead of hurting them.

13

JOKES AND TEASING: WHEN ARE THEY FUNNY AND WHEN ARE THEY NOT

> *Let there be no filthiness nor foolish talk nor crude joking, which are out of place, but instead let there be thanksgiving.*
>
> — *EPHESIANS 5:4 ESV*

QUESTION: What is the one place where Christmas comes before Thanksgiving?

ANSWER: The dictionary!

It's okay. You can laugh. You know you want to. Why wouldn't you? It's a corny-sort-of-funny-joke. But not all jokes are funny. They aren't even actual jokes.

Does *Diary of a Whimpy Kid* sound familiar? Have you ever been the one to dare or shame somebody into getting their tongue stuck on the frozen flagpole like Ralphie did? Do you laugh at jokes at someone else's expense? Do you tell the same kind of jokes? What about cussing? What about bullying kids who are different from you?

FYI: You are just as different to *them,* as they are to you. Think about that!

Cussing, bullying, teasing, jokes that aren't really jokes—there is no room in your life for things like this. None.

CASE IN POINT

If you look in Genesis 17:16-17 God told Abraham that he and his wife, Sarah, would have a baby, Abraham thought it was a joke because they were both in their nineties! It was crazy to think she could have a baby. God was not messing around though; He had a plan.

Jonah thought God's command to go to the dirty, crime-ridden city of Nineveh was a joke. A bad one. There was no way God wanted Jonah to try to turn *those* people around. Did He? They weren't worth saving. Were they?

It didn't take long for Jonah to learn an important lesson about God's character. It's one you need to learn, too. GOD DOESN'T JOKE AROUND. This doesn't mean God doesn't have a sense of humor or that He never laughs. Some of the things He created—things like fireflies, giraffes, and manatees—prove He has a sense of humor. You and I are created in God's image, which means we have bits and pieces of God's character in us—including a sense of humor. But when God speaks, He means business. When God spoke to people back then and in all the words He speaks through in The Holy Bible, He means business. It's no joke. He's not teasing. He's not being a bully. He says what needs to be said and He says it all for one reason only. Love.

USE IT FOR YOU

1: What do you say or how do you treat people who are different from you—the kids who are usually picked last or made fun of because of something that shouldn't even matter?

2: Have you ever been teased or bullied because you are one of those kids? How did it make you feel? What did you do?

3: What do you do when someone starts telling dirty jokes, bullying someone, or when teasing gets out of hand?

4: What do you think makes a joke dirty or bad? When do you think teasing turns into bullying?

5: Do your answers to question 4 agree with what God says in the Bible? If not, are you ready to change your mind so that you agree with God? Why or why not?

MORE FROM THE BIBLE

Look up the following verses. Read each one and think about what it is saying to YOU.

- Psalm 82:4
- Matthew 7:12
- Luke 6:45

PRAYER PROMPT

Pray for courage to walk away from conversations you shouldn't be part of and courage to say no to cussing, dirty jokes, and bullying.

Pray for courage to stand up for yourself if someone bullies you.

14

AUTHORITY DESERVES YOUR RESPECT

Let every person be subject to the governing authorities. For there is no authority except from God, and those that exist have been instituted by God.

— *ROMANS 13:1 ESV*

Respect and disrespect for authority is something we hear a lot about on the news, at school, and just about everywhere else we go. Showing respect for authority is a problem for basically everyone – kids and adults alike It doesn't have to be a problem for you, though. In fact, you can be part of the solution. By taking a knee to God you give God the honor, love, and respect He deserves. It also gives Him authority over your life, which is never a bad idea because He always makes the best choices and decisions for you.

Do you remember what Jesus said when He told the people how to pray? He said that we are supposed to pray that His Will, not ours, will be done on Earth as it is in Heaven (Matthew 6:9–10). You know what that means, don't you? When you pray that way you are literally saying that you are willing to do things God's way and follow His plan for your life because you know it will be way better than what you can come up with on your own.

Does this mean people in authority are always right? No, except God. Does it mean you should never ask questions or speak up when something doesn't feel right? No, not at all. But it should always be done gracefully. Disagreeing with authority is not the same as disrespecting authority. You have every right to disagree with authority, and even take action to challenge it as long as you don't break the law or rules, which is the same as doing it *respectfully*.

One last thing to keep in mind before we look at examples of this from the Bible: God loves you and everyone else enough to let Jesus die for our sins. Remembering that important piece of truth will go a long way when it comes to respecting people in authority, and everyone else too.

CASE IN POINT

We're going to talk about David and Daniel again because they are great examples of what a guy who loves God says, does, and acts.

David was anointed king by Samuel about ten years before he actually *became* the king. Here, anointed is a fancy way of saying

God chose David to be king and sent Samuel to tell him and his dad. The reason he had to wait so long was because Saul was already king. King Saul was a rotten person and a rotten leader. One thing that made him so rotten was his hatred of David. Earlier I mentioned that King Saul spent more time trying to kill David than he did taking care of regular "king stuff".

Put yourself in David's shoes. If you knew you were going to be king, and the current king was trying to kill you, and you had the ability to outsmart the king and kill him, what would you do? Would you do what David did, which was to wait his turn? In 1 Samuel 22:1–2, David made sure he and his friends stayed a few steps ahead of King Saul, but he waited until Saul died because he respected God's authority. Afterall, God chose Saul to be king and David respected Saul's position as king.

Daniel was a kid who was going places. David was one of Daniel's ancestors, so that made Daniel part of the royal family. He was smart, had a great personality, he was good looking, and he was the kind of guy who wasn't afraid to speak up, but he always did it without being disrespectful. All of this came in handy when the Babylonians came in and took over the entire Israelite nation. The king of Babylon, Nebuchadnezzar, and his righthand guys were so impressed with Daniel and three of his friends that they offered them important jobs in the new government (Daniel 1).

Most people would give that offer a big, fat no. No way would they work for the guy that wrecked their country and hauled them off to live somewhere else. But not Daniel. He took the job. But when he was told to do some things that contradicted

God's laws, Daniel said, "No, thank you" (Daniel 1:8) He was confident, humble, and respectful—actions that showed his commitment to God. Daniel 2:1–49 highlights Daniel's wisdom and faithfulness, as well as Nebuchadnezzar's reliance on God and recognition of His power.

USE IT FOR YOU

1: Have you ever disrespected someone in authority? If so, how did doing so make you feel?

2: Do you think people at your school are disrespectful to the teachers? Why or why not?

3: What are some things you can do to be more respectful to set an example for your friends?

4: What about your parents or grandparents? How are you doing when it comes to respecting their authority? What would change if you were more respectful to them?

MORE FROM THE BIBLE

Look up the following verses. Read each one and think about what it is saying to YOU.

- 1 Timothy 2:1–4
- Romans 13:7
- Romans 13:2
- Ephesians 6:1

PRAYER PROMPT

Pray for an attitude of respect for others, especially those in authority, and pray for courage to set a good example in this for your friends and peers.

15

THE POSITIVE AND NEGATIVE POLES OF PEER PRESSURE

> *And Jesus answered them, "See that no one leads you astray."*
>
> — *MATTHEW 24:4 ESV*

Picture this: church camp (yes, church camp) 2013. Micah was "that guy"—the guy who was lagging behind when it comes to what teenage boys are interested in. While the rest of the fifteen- and sixteen-year-old guys were into sports, girls, cars, thinking about college, and working part-time jobs, Micah still played with action figures and was more concerned about the possibility of a real Starship Enterprise than driving an actual car. When they played capture the flag, he was sporting night-vision goggles pretending he was on another plant instead of helping his team. Yet everyone liked Micah. What wasn't to like? He was funny, nice, and smart. He was so nice he would have eaten dirt before hurting anyone's feelings. So, what's the problem you ask? And what does this have to do with peer pressure? The problem was a guy we'll call Eric.

This was Eric's first time at church camp. He and his mom had moved to the area to be closer to his grandparents after she and Eric's dad got a divorce. He didn't want to be there, but his grandparents had insisted on it.

Right from the start Eric picked on Micah by making fun of him. Eric tried to humiliate and embarrass Micah but, almost as quickly, the other kids let Eric know that wasn't going to fly. Eric didn't see why it was such a big deal. Guys like Micah were asking for it, right? But Eric was also smart enough to figure out that if he didn't stop, it would be a long and miserable week at camp.

Fast-forward to Friday. Eric still wasn't sure about all the Bible stuff, praying, and all the rest of the God stuff they threw at him, but he had had more fun than he ever thought he would. The kids were nice, especially Micah. Micah knew everything there is to know about the St. Louis Cardinals. And the food... the food was great!

This is a great example of positive peer pressure. Eric followed the lead of the other campers and ended up learning some important lessons and making a ton of new friends. It doesn't always work that way, though, does it? Sometimes peer pressure works in the exact opposite way.

Let's investigate Sam's example of negative peer pressure. Sam was one of the captains of the varsity soccer team. It was the last home game of the season. The team thought it would be fun to change and grab a snack at Sam's house before returning to campus for the game. Some of the guys found a liquor bottle and thought it would be funny to get tipsy before the game since they were playing a major underdog. Sam knew this was a bad idea and wanted to play hard for the last game no matter what the other team's stats were. He refused to take part until the pressure from his teammates became too strong. Sam eventually caved.

During the warm-up drills the boys' sweat started to reek of alcohol and the whole team was caught. Not only did Sam's team have to forfeit the game, but they were all suspended immediately for underage drinking, being under the influence on campus, and for drunk driving. The punishment could have been much worse.

CASE IN POINT

Zacchaeus, the short, wealthy tax collector is a guy who gives us a positive spin on peer pressure. In Luke 19:1–10, he noticed how different (in a good way) Jesus' followers were, so he followed *them* straight to Jesus and even climbed a tree to get a glimpse of Jesus. Zacchaeus was so moved by Jesus's presence, that he completely changed his life around and relinquished his wealth to the poor.

On the other hand, Pilate let peer pressure steer him in the opposite direction. In Matthew 27:24–25, he knew Jesus wasn't guilty of anything the Pharisees accused him of. Pilate knew Jesus hadn't done anything worse than make people feel guilty for the way they acted and treated other people. But he caved to the peer pressure of the crowd. He let them bully him into sending Jesus to his death.

USE IT FOR YOU

1: When have you let peer pressure lead you in the wrong direction? Why did you follow these people, and what happened?

2: When have you let peer pressure lead you in the right direction? Why did you follow these people and what happened?

3: Is there a situation where you witnessed negative peer pressure? What was the outcome? Is there anything you would do differently if it happened again?

4: What are some things you can do to be a better peer?

MORE FROM THE BIBLE

Look up the following verses. Read each one and think about what it is saying to YOU.

- Proverbs 13:20
- Galatians 1:10
- Psalm 1
- Matthew 7:12

PRAYER PROMPT

Ask God to give you the courage to do what is right under pressure and to treat people the way you want to be treated.

16

FORGIVENESS IS FOR YOU

> *For if you forgive men when they sin against you, your heavenly Father will also forgive you. But if you do not forgive men their sins, your Father will not forgive your sins.*
>
> — *MATTHEW* 6:14–1

Forgiveness is for YOU. Even if the person you forgive doesn't know or care, you know you are doing what God wants, and that's what matters.

Charles knows all about that. He spent the first fifteen years of his life with parents who were physically, emotionally, and mentally abusive. He did a good job of hiding things. There were times when school lunch was the only meal he ate for days at a time. He made up excuses when the teachers asked how he busted his lip and why he didn't get stitches. He did his best to write with his left hand when his right arm was too swollen, bruised, and throbbing with pain to hold a pencil.

Kids who are abused like Charles often grow up to be abusers. But not Charles. Charles was a good student because he loved school. School was a safe place. A place where he could laugh, play, and where he learned that what happened at home was not his fault. Charles also found a friend and father-figure, his shop teacher, Mr. B. Mr. B and his wife started taking Charles to church and finding every reason they could to keep Charles out of his house.

Today, Charles is a solid Christian. Most people would never guess Charles had such a lousy childhood. He is a loving husband and dad, and an officer in the United States Marine Corps. because he decided to forgive his parents. He forgave them because he didn't want the anger and resentment, he had for them to keep him from being the best person he could be.

Forgiveness is for YOU. If Charles can forgive, so can you. Even if the person you forgive doesn't know or care, you know you are doing what God wants, and that's what matters. Your future home in Heaven depends on it.

CASE IN POINT

Do the names Jacob and Esau sound familiar? They were the twin sons of Isaac and Rebecca. Abraham and Sarah were their grandparents mentioned in Genesis 25. Esau was born a few minutes before Jacob, which meant Esau was technically the oldest. But Rebecca loved Jacob more than she loved Esau, which definitely takes her out of the running for any "Best Mom" award. But we're not here to talk about that.

What we are going to talk about, is the way she and Jacob plotted against Esau and Isaac. They tricked both into giving Jacob all the rights and privileges of being the oldest son. And back in those days, that was a *really big deal. a reeeeeeeeeeeally big deal.*

Jacob ended up running away, sort of. He went to live in Rebecca's hometown, ended up marrying her nieces—two sisters named Leah and Rachel. Again, that's a whole other story for another time.

Anyway, after living with his in-laws for several years, Jacob took his wives and children, packed up all their stuff, rounded up all their livestock, and headed back to where he had come from. It was quite a scene. A bunch of people, hundreds and hundreds of sheep, camels, cattle, and all their worldly possessions, hiking and riding for miles and miles and miles...

The news spread pretty quickly, and it wasn't long before Esau found out. Almost immediately, he sent a message to Jacob, saying he was anxious to see him. Jacob panicked. He just knew Esau was going to get even with him, maybe even kidnap or kill members of his family! But that's not what happened.

Esau was extremely happy to see Jacob. He gave him gift after gift. He told him how much he'd missed him and congratulated him on being such a huge success (Jacob was super rich at that point).

Jacob didn't know what to think. When he could no longer stand the suspense, he asked, "What's up? You do remember what I did to you, don't you?"

Esau said that of course he remembered, but that it didn't matter anymore. He said, "I've had a great life. I am rich, I love my family, I have lots of land and livestock. What you did was wrong, but it didn't ruin my life." Esau went on to say that he had forgiven Jacob long ago, because he didn't want to waste his time and energy on being angry.

The twist to this true story plot is that God had chosen Jacob before he and Esau were even born, to be the father (the beginning) of the Israelite nation. Esau's people ended up being the Israelites' enemies. But when it comes to forgiveness, Esau got it right.

USE IT FOR YOU

1: Are you holding a grudge against anyone? Write their name(s) below and a sentence explaining why you are having a hard time forgiving them.

2: There is an old saying that goes like this: "Forgive and forget." People say they cannot forgive someone because they cannot forget what that person did to them. It's true—our brains hold on to things, especially the bad things with really intense negative emotions. But remember that forgiving someone is not the same as reconciling with that person. It simply means that you release them from their wrong against you. So, here's the question: can you forgive the names above and release them from their wrong against you?

3: Is someone holding a grudge against you? Why? Be the guy God wants you to be—go to that person and ask them to forgive you. Ask if there is anything you can do to make it right. If they do...great! If they don't, that's on them. You can go forward knowing you did the right thing.

4: What do you think about the *fact* that God won't forgive you if you don't forgive people who hurt or do mean things to you (Matthew 6:14–15)?

MORE FROM THE BIBLE

Look up the following verses. Read each one and think about what it is saying to YOU.

- Ephesians 4:32
- Colossians 3:13

PRAYER PROMPT

Prayer for God to give you an attitude of forgiveness. Ask God to remind you every single day that grudges are wrong and that it isn't up to us to get even with people who hurt us. That's God's job.

17

OWN IT

> *A man finds joy in an apt reply—and how good is a timely word.*
>
> — *PROVERBS 15:23*

How many times have your parents said something like:

- "You might still get in trouble for doing something you shouldn't, but as long as you tell the truth, it won't be near as bad as if you lie to me."
- "The worst thing you can do is lie to me."
- "As long as you own your mistakes, that's all it is—a mistake. But if you don't own it, that's the same as lying, and liars cannot be trusted."

That's what Proverbs 15:23 is talking about. Words like "apt reply" and "timely word" sound a little funny or weird to us, but that's the way they talked back then. If King Solomon would have written that verse last week, he probably would have said something like this...

A person always feels better when they admit their mistakes, when they speak up for what's right, and when they don't try to hide the truth.

Owning up to your mistakes doesn't mean you are dumb or that it's too late to do the right thing. Making mistakes doesn't make you a failure, either. Think about it—if Thomas Edison wouldn't have owned his mistakes and worked to correct them, you could be reading this by candlelight. What would have happened to Michael Jordan if he decided to give up basketball after he was cut from the team his sophomore year of high school? He could have easily quit after his coach thought he wasn't good enough to play.

When you look at people like Edison and Jordan it is easy to see that owning up to our setbacks is an important step toward reaching your potential.

CASE IN POINT

In the Book of Job, God gave the Devil permission to try to get Job to ditch his faith and love for God. I know—it sounds crazy, but it's true. The only reason God allowed the Devil to do it, is because He knew Job could handle it. Poor Job! It must have been awful for him. He lost everything he owned and everyone he loved, except his wife.

Job tried his best to not let it get to him. He knew God was in control. He knew God loved him. He knew God has the right to do whatever He wants. But Job was lower than low, and he accused God of making mistakes. Mistake number one: creating Job. Mistake number two: letting Job enjoy such a great life...and then taking it all away. Mistake number three: keeping Job alive and totally miserable. Why was it a mistake for Job to say these things? Because nothing God does is a mistake, and God didn't waste any time letting Job know that.

In the last few chapters of the book of Job, God calls Job out by asking him if *he* knew how to contain the oceans between the shores, if *he* knew every time a wild animal gives birth, if *he* could make the sun rise and set, and a whole bunch of other things. Job got the message loud and clear. And then he did exactly what God wanted him to do—Job owned his mistakes, apologized, asked forgiveness, and moved on.

You asked, 'Who is this that obscures my counsel without knowledge?' Surely I spoke of things I did not understand, things too wonderful for me to know...My ears had heard of you but now my eyes have seen you.

—JOB 42:3 AND 5 NIV

USE IT FOR YOU

1: Which of the following do you do most often when you make a mistake:

- Own your mistake, fix it, and move on
- Ignore it and hope it will go away or fix itself
- Deny you did anything wrong
- Blame it on someone or something else

2: Think about some of the mistakes you have made but didn't own up to. How would owning and correcting them changed what happened?

3: Have you ever been blamed for something you didn't do? How did it make you feel? What did you do about it?

4: Name three good things that can come from owning up to a setback?

5: Do you agree or disagree with this statement and explain your answer: Denying your mistakes is the same as lying.

MORE FROM THE BIBLE

Look up the following verses. Read each one and think about what it is saying to YOU.

- James 3:9–12
- James 1:19

PRAYER PROMPT

Pray that God will help you use your mistakes to make you a better person. Pray that you will not be too proud or scared to admit your mistakes and learn from them.

18

MAN UP!

> *He has showed you, O man, what is good. And what does the LORD require of you? To act justly and to love mercy and to walk humbly with your God.*
>
> — *MICAH 6:8 NIV*

Real men don't cry. Real men don't wear pink. Real men watch football. Real men don't let anyone get to them. Real men take what is coming to them. Real men don't take "no" for an answer. Real men don't need to ask for directions. Real men don't ask for help. Real men don't show their emotions. That's what the world says, anyway.

SPOILER ALERT!!!! It's all a lie. A big, fat, whopper lie. *Real* men cry, can wear pink if they want to, don't have to watch football, don't bully people to get what they want, and they aren't afraid to ask for help or directions. *Real* men know how to say "no" and respect people who say "no" to them. *Real* men own up to their emotions and aren't afraid to learn to keep them under control or express how they feel.

It's not always easy to know who to believe, is it? Sometimes it is easier to believe what you hear and see on social media, the movies, what your friends, or coaches say than what you read in the Bible and hear at church. It is easier because the people telling the lies are loud and all around you. They make it sound more fun, but they also make you feel guilty or wimpy if you aren't that kind of guy.

It's enough to make a guy want to climb the nearest tree and not come down. Or slap on some headphones and block everything out. But before you decided to do either one, keep reading. There is another option—one that actually works.

CASE IN POINT

King Solomon had it all—all the wealth, popularity, power, respect, and intelligence a guy could have. But do you know where it all came from? Why he had those things? God gave it all to him. In 1 Kings 3:5–14, God asked Solomon which of the following three things he wanted—wisdom, wealth, or power. Solomon chose wisdom. And because he chose wisdom, God gave him the other two as "bonus blessings."

Solomon got caught up in the lies and temptations the Devil put in front of him 24/7. He lost his faith in God and put his faith in other things, including himself…for a while. As Solomon got older, he got wiser (again). He took a long, hard look at his life and decided he didn't like what he saw. Solomon realized that what mattered most was to live a life that put God first, always.

When you stop and think about it, it makes perfect sense. God created you, so why wouldn't He know exactly what is best for you? Why wouldn't He know what makes you a real man and what doesn't? The greatest leaders of the Bible put God first. God made your emotions, it's part of being human. He also designed you with the ability to use logic and reason. Every great leader not only knows how to express themselves to their peers but how to navigate the rough waters calmly and effectively. The only way to truly do this is by having full faith and trust in God.

USE IT FOR YOU

1: Who do you look up to as an example of what it means to be a man?

2: What have you learned from this person (or people)?

3: What lies about being a man do you have the hardest time *not* believing? Why?

4: Read Ecclesiastes 11:9 and rewrite it in your own words.

MORE FROM THE BIBLE

Look up the following verses. Read each one and think about what it is saying to YOU.

- Ecclesiastes 12:13–14
- Genesis 1:26
- Psalm 119:9
- Hebrews 13:7

PRAYER PROMPT

Ask God to give you Godly men who will mentor you and hold you accountable for being a real man.

19

A TEDDY BEAR KIND OF GUY

But the fruit of the Spirit is love, joy, peace, patience, kindness, goodness, faithfulness, gentleness, and self-control. Against such things there is no law.

— *GALATIANS 5:22–23 NIV*

Have you ever seen the old television show, M*A*S*H? If you have, you already know about Radar. If you haven't seen it, ask your parents about it. I'm sure they have, and they will vouch for what I'm about to say.

M*A*S*H was a sitcom about a mobile army surgical hospital. One of the main characters was a humble corporal, Radar (Walter) O'Reilly. He was a young, naïve farm boy from Iowa who didn't cuss, or drink and he never had a girlfriend...and he still slept with his teddy bear. Radar was also the company clerk. In Army talk, that means he was the guy who kept the place running smoothly (or as smooth as an Army hospital in the middle of a warzone can be). He was true-blue loyal to the colonel, who was the commander of the unit. Colonel Potter was a solid leader, but even he depended on Radar to make sure everything was in tip-top shape.

But a teddy bear? Really? Yep. That bear was his most trusted confidant, and he couldn't sleep without it. Not the kind of thing you would expect from someone in the Army, is it? You also wouldn't think a guy with a teddy bear would be capable of doing all the things Radar did. But he was, which proves that you don't have to be rough, tough, and gruff to be strong and dependable. You can have a soft heart with nerves of steel and a brilliant mind. That combination is what makes you the kind of guy who can love people, just the way Jesus does.

CASE IN POINT

When Jesus preached his sermon on the mount in Matthew 5:1–12, He instructed us to be meek, which means to be calm, humble, and respectful. Later in that same sermon, He warned us not to mistreat people because of the way they look, where they come from, or how much money they have.

Do you remember a few chapters ago when you learned that the humblest man on earth was Moses (Numbers 12:3)? Yet Moses went toe to toe with Pharaoh and led hundreds of thousands of Israelites – grumbling, whinny, ungrateful Israelites – across the desert to the border of the land God promised to give them.

And what about Paul (formerly Saul)? He was highly respected and popular with the Christians around the world, but he also suffered beatings, nasty jail cells, threats on his life, and accused of crimes he didn't commit, because he wouldn't back away from preaching the Gospel so that countless people could become Christians, too. And he did it willingly. It would take a while to count all the times Paul says he is honored to be able to suffer for Jesus. In 1 Corinthians 9:22 he said he didn't care what he had to go through if it meant even one more person would be saved.

"To the weak I became weak, to win the weak. I have become all things to all people so that by all possible means I might save some."

USE IT FOR YOU

1: If someone asked you to define the words 'humble' and 'meek' what would you say?

2: Have you ever made fun of someone or treated them differently because you thought they were weak for showing their emotions? When and why?

3: Have you ever wanted to help someone but didn't because you were afraid someone would make fun of you for it? Who did you want to help and why?

4: Write down the names of two or three famous people (from the past or present) and two or three personal friends or family members you think are humble. Next to each name, write a sentence or two explaining why you think they are humble.

MORE FROM THE BIBLE

Look up the following verses. Read each one and think about what it is saying to YOU.

- Matthew 23:12
- Proverbs 11:2
- James 4:10

PRAYER PROMPT

Pray that you won't be afraid or embarrassed to be humble and compassionate—that you won't be afraid to help people in need.

Pray that you will not be afraid or embarrassed to cry, admit you are scared, to ask for help or a hug, and to be there for people when they feel the same.

20

THE INTEGRITY CHALLENGE

> *The LORD said to Satan, "Have you considered my servant, Job? There is no one on earth like him; he is blameless and upright, a man who fears God and shuns evil. And he still maintains his integrity, though you incited me against him to ruin him without any reason."*
>
> — *JOB 2:3 NIV*

Let's start off by defining what exactly integrity is or what does it mean to be a person of integrity. According to Webster's definition of integrity, it means to possess the qualities of being honest and having strong moral principles, the state of being complete or whole, or being in an unimpaired condition. So, in other words it means to be incorruptible, to be of sound mind and body, and undivided.

Chase and Brian have been best friends since kindergarten. But when Chase made the varsity baseball team their freshman year in high school, he started hanging around the rest of the team. They were all older and most of them were into partying and drinking. Chase thought it was cool to be invited to hang out with them. But Brian warned him that if he wasn't careful, Chase would end up in trouble and doing things he knew he shouldn't do. Chase brushed him off and accused Brian of just being jealous.

By the start of their sophomore year, Chase spent most weekends getting drunk with his baseball "friends." Brian tried to stop him, but Chase still wouldn't listen. Then one Friday night, the first Friday night Chase had his driver's license, he came to the football game with alcohol on his breath. Brian couldn't believe it! He didn't care how mad Chase got, he was not going to let his best friend drink and drive. He might kill himself or someone else!

Brian took Chase's keys (he had to knock him down to get them), then called Chase's dad, told him what had been going on, and basically told his dad he needed to come and get the slightly drunk Chase. Chase was furious at Brian and swore he would get even and that he would never forgive Brian for what he'd done. Brain remained steadfast and unapologetic. He was not going to be divided based on what he knew the right thing to do was or what he thought Chase would want him to do.

Chase's dad was disappointed and angry with Chase and didn't waste any time doing what he believed was best to keep his son safe. He also told Chase that he was one lucky guy to have friend like Brian – a friend that cared enough to do what was right for Chase no matter what.

“Brian is a guy with integrity,” Chase’s dad said. “I hope you realize that before it’s too late.”

It took a couple of years for Chase to realize that Brian had saved him from ruining his life, especially since he got kicked off the baseball team because he got caught drinking. But he finally forgave him and admitted he was in over his head. Brian and Chase are now almost thirty. They never did go back to being as close as they were before Chase joined the baseball team, but they still hang out occasionally. Now Chase will tell you straight up that if he ever has a problem, a tough decision to make, or needs a reality check, Brian is the first person he calls, and the only one he trusts to tell him what he needs to hear.

CASE IN POINT

The guy we’re going to talk about isn’t even mentioned by name in the Bible, but he’s a fantastic example of what integrity looks like. Here’s the short version of the event….

In 2 Kings 5, Naaman was a successful and popular commander in the army of Aram. He was living life large until he got leprosy. Leprosy was highly contagious and incurable. Anyone who had it was usually sent to live in a leprosy camp, but for some reason, Naaman didn’t do that. Instead, he sent a servant guy to find the prophet, Elisha. Why Elisha? Because even though Naaman didn’t worship or even really care about God, he had seen and heard about some of the amazing things God had done and everyone knew God used Elisha to do a lot of the things he did. Naaman also respected the obvious power God had, so he wanted Elisha to ask God to get rid of his leprosy.

The servant found Elisha and asked him what Naaman should do. Elisha said that if Naaman would dunk himself in the Jordan River seven times, he would be healed. So, the servant guy made a mad dash back to Naaman and told him what he should do. Naaman was not impressed. He was angry! The Jordan River was a nasty, dirty river and in his opinion, to do that was undignified for someone as important and powerful as he was.

This is where the servant guy's integrity comes into play. This servant guy was an Israelite who worshipped and loved God. So, even though he was the lowest man on the ladder and Naaman was his boss and commander in the army, he spoke up and said what needed to be said. He said, "...if the prophet had told you to do some great thing, would you not have done it? How much more, then, when he tells you, 'Wash and be cleansed'!" Or, in words you might understand a little better, the servant guy said, "If Elisha would have told you to do something bold or exciting, you would have jumped on it. So why not this? Do you want to be healed, or not?" You know what? Naaman realized the servant guy was right. So, he dunked himself in the river seven times, and by the seventh time, he was completely healed.

That took guts. Not Naaman, but the servant guy. It also took faith—not in Elisha, but in God. If this unnamed servant wouldn't have been a guy of integrity, it's doubtful Naaman would have dunked himself and been healed.

USE IT FOR YOU

1: Name three things most people think are okay or normal, but you know God doesn't approve of them.

2: How can you speak up about these things to let people know God doesn't approve?

3: Take a minute to think about what it means to have integrity. What grade would you give yourself? FYI: Someone who has integrity is sincere, honest, reliable, respectful.

4: List three things you can do to be a guy who has a lot of integrity.

MORE FROM THE BIBLE

Look up the following verses. Read each one and think about what it is saying to YOU.

- Proverbs 10:9
- Proverbs 12:22
- 2 Corinthians 8:21

PRAYER PROMPT

Pray that you will always think before you act and speak, so that you will do and say what is right and honors God.

21

YOU ARE WORTH ALL OF THAT AND MORE

> *When I consider your heavens, the work of your fingers, the moon and the stars, which you have set in place, what is man that you are mindful of him, the son of man that you care for him?*
>
> — PSALM 8:3–4 NIV

If we are being bold, we need to say that when it comes to talking about self-confidence, self-esteem, and self-respect, people usually spend most of their time and energy talking to girls. Why? Because girls struggle with it more than guys do. But that doesn't mean it is never a problem for guys, so let's talk about it.

Guys don't like waking up to a zit on their face any more than girls do. Guys are just as afraid of tripping over something and sending their lunch tray flying through the air as girls are. Guys break out in a sweat when that cute girl from class looks at them or says hi, just like girls do. Guys think about things like grades, making varsity vs. junior varsity, peer pressure to drink, do drugs, or have sex, just like girls do. Guys don't always get along with their parents, they have arguments with their friends, and get way too caught up in social media just like girls do.

The difference between you and the girls is the way you deal with it. Girls put it all out there for everyone to hear, see, and comment about (most of the time, anyway). Guys tend to keep it all locked up inside and put on a tough guy act to keep it from somehow getting loose. That can't happen because if it does, everyone will know what a loser you are. Right?

Wrong!

The reality for everyone, girls and guys alike, is that none of these things make you a loser. None of these things make you dumb, ugly, incompetent, or worthless. Every single one of the things you worry and stress over is normal adolescent and teenage stuff. It's life.

The good news is that it gets better. It won't be too long before you realize none of these things is as big a deal as you think they are now. At least it can get better…if you allow yourself to realize that there is nothing wrong with the way God made you. Or like a friend of mine always tells the kids she teaches, "God don't make no junk!" That's right—God don't make junk, so you aren't junk. You are valuable to God just the way you are. So valuable that He put His Son through a brutal and horrible death *so that* you could be his son, too.

CASE IN POINT

The Bible gives us lots of examples of people who didn't have much (or any) self-confidence and people who didn't always understand or remember that we humans are the only thing God created that he called "very good" instead of just good. People like…

- In 1 Kings 18:19–21, Elijah who was on the run from wicked King Ahab and Queen Jezebel. He felt sure he wasn't important enough to God for God to take care of him. God proved him wrong in a big way (lots of big ways, actually). God gave Elijah a safe place to hide, water to drink, and food to eat, when everyone else had none because of a drought.
- In Acts 9:3–6, while Paul was still Saul, he was a Christian hater and hunter. He hunted them down to throw them in prison, beat them up, and let them be killed. When Jesus spoke to Paul from heaven, Paul had a hard time believing Jesus would want him for anything. After everything he'd done *to* followers of Jesus, he couldn't understand why Jesus would want him to be one. When Jesus talked to him from Heaven, ignoring Him wasn't really an option. Paul decided if Jesus thought he was worth talking to, he needed to listen and obey. So, that's what he did.
- John the Baptist is another great example of learning why it is okay to be confident and proud of your accomplishments and abilities. In case you don't remember (or haven't heard), John the Baptist was Jesus'

> cousin (Mary and John's mom, Elizabeth were cousins). John the Baptist was chosen by God to set the stage for Jesus. He told people God was getting ready to send them the Savior. So, in Matthew 3:16–17 when Jesus arrived on the scene, He told John to baptize Him. John's gut reaction was to say no. Not because he didn't want to, but because *he didn't think or feel up to the task. He didn't think he was worthy* (good enough) to do such an important job. Jesus told him he was, John listened, obeyed, and God was pleased.

NOTE: If you know the rest of the story, you know John the Baptist was killed by wicked King Herod after John called him out for sinning. This might make you think that God wasn't watching out for John—that he didn't bless John for his faith and obedience. It's easy to see why you might think that, but it's not true, and we will talk about that in the next chapter.

USE IT FOR YOU

1: Have you ever wanted to speak up about God stuff but didn't because you were afraid you would mess up? Or not be able to answer someone's question? What did you do instead of speaking up?

2: Write ten words to describe what you like most about yourself. Don't be shy. You are not bragging. You are letting God know you appreciate the work He put into creating you.

3: What do you want to be when you are an adult? How can you use your job and your talents to let people know how great God is?

4: Are there people who make you feel bad about yourself? What can you do to avoid them and not let them get to you? Are there things you do and places you go that make you feel bad about yourself? What can you do to quit doing these things or going to these places?

5: Memorize Psalms 139:14 and believe it!

MORE FROM THE BIBLE

Look up the following verses. Read each one and think about what it is saying to YOU.

- Proverbs 3:6
- Joshua 1:9
- John 3:16–17

PRAYER PROMPT

Ask God to help you live your most authentic self and to walk confidently in any social situation. Thank Him for giving you Jesus. Ask Him to help you believe without a shadow of doubt that you can do all the things He created you to do.

22

WHAT IS GOD THINKING?

> *Count it all joy, my brothers, when you meet trials of various kinds, for you know that the testing of your faith produces steadfastness.*
>
> — *JAMES 1:2–3 ESV*

Have you ever done that thing with dominos—that thing where you line them up just so, tap the one on the end, then watch them all fall, one at a time in near-perfect rhythm? That one single action affected all the dominos. That one choice you made to tip a single domino changed everything.

Life is full of what we call domino effects: a single choice or decision that effects a whole lot of other events. You might be reflecting now on your life, both bad choices and good ones were domino effects for the situation you are in now.

A couple examples:

Let's say you decided to be brave and join a new school club and through your involvement you meet a whole new set of friends who share your interests. These friends introduce you to new experiences, such as attending events related to the club. You gain new skills and develop a sense of confidence and purpose through your involvement. This newfound confidence leads you to set higher goals for yourself academically and personally. You work hard with improved grades and increased opportunities. As graduation approaches, you get accepted into a great college that aligns with your interest and purpose, then you go on to have a successful and fulfilling career in a field that you love surrounded by awesome people. All stemming from a choice to try something new and having full faith that God had your back.

On the other hand, let's say you make the bad choice to go 4-wheeling with your friends, you get too rowdy, wreck the 4-wheeler, and end up with broken bones, which means you fall behind in school, which means you must go to summer school to catch up, which means you....

See how that works?

But here's something else you need to think about. When something bad happens, it doesn't always have to stay bad. Sometimes "bad" things that happen end up being for our own good.

Colin knows all about that. While he and his family were on vacation, they went to an amusement park with all sorts of crazy, wild, fast rides. He was having a great time. His sister was, too…until she got sick from riding so many rides. Colin's parents insisted they stay together, which meant he was going to have to wait a while to ride the wildest rollercoaster in the park. He wasn't happy about it. At all. Why did his sister have to get sick and ruin all the fun!?

But, while he was impatiently waiting for his parents to let him get in line, the ride broke down and everyone on it was stuck in the air…in the heat…some of them upside down…for over an hour.

See how that works? Colin thought having to wait to ride the rollercoaster was a bad thing. Turns out it was anything but bad.

You and I know there are a lot worse things in life than not riding a roller coaster. People we love get sick and die. Pets die. Sometimes we must move away and leave all our friends behind. We don't always make the team. Friends lie to us. People at school bully us. Life is full of heavy things, BUT…

Through God you can overcome any adversity. These "bad things" or difficult situations can be looked at as an invitation to draw closer to God. Keep your heart full of gratitude no matter what. Develop a habit of turning to prayer for all things, good and bad, this will lead to a life joy. If you put God in charge, the domino effect of bad things will work out for the best. After all, God knows everything there is to know about you and He loves you more than you can imagine.

Always.

CASE IN POINT

We've talked about Joseph before. Here's a guy that knew all about bad things turning out for the best. In Genesis 37:28, his brothers beat him up and sold him (bad thing), but he ended up being the head guy in Egypt (good thing).

Here's another example, the gossips about Mary and Joseph had to be intense! They were engaged to be married but not fully married yet according to the tradition back then, and to be pregnant already?! Even Joseph was having second thoughts about Mary (Mathew 1:21). It doesn't take much of an imagination to think about how everyone pointed fingers at them, stopped talking to them, and treated them like they were pond scum (bad thing). Mary and Joseph stayed faithful and obedient to God even when they did not fully understand. God blessed them by giving them the honor and privilege of being Jesus' earthly parents (good thing).

The Israelites were just captured and exiled. They were in a strange land called Babylon and feeling lost and depressed. A famous prophet by the name of Jeremiah wrote this verse to comfort them, a friendly reminder that God is always in control and that He has a good plan. Jeremiah instructed them to settle in and start planting roots because they were going to be there for a while. But even in their waiting, God was with them and had a plan that would lead them to prosperity and peace and to never forget that God is always with you. Here is the verse:

For I know the plans I have for you," declares the Lord, "plans to prosper you and not to harm you, plans to give you hope and a future.

It's easier to see the domino of events looking back on this true history from where we are sitting. I know it is sometimes hard to look at your life in the present moment and see the string of events that God has laid out for you and where it could be leading. We never truly know where it could be leading. That is exactly what Jeremiah was saying. Have full trust and faith in God and know that the plans for you are good.

USE IT FOR YOU

1: What would you say is the worst thing that has ever happened to you that wasn't the consequence of a choice or decision you made?

2: Can you think of anything God has done to bring something good out of this event? If so, what? If not, start praying. Ask God to help you want to believe and see the good He can do even when you are going through a tough time.

3: What would you say is the worst thing that has ever happened to you because of a poor choice or decision you made?

4: Can you think of anything God has done to bring something good out of this event? If so, what? If not, start praying. Ask God to help you believe and see that it is possible.

5: Why do you think God takes the time to turn bad situations into something good?

MORE FROM THE BIBLE

Look up the following verses. Read each one and think about what it is saying to YOU.

- Jeremiah 29:11
- Psalm 37:5
- John 16:33

PRAYER PROMPT

Ask God to help you make wise choices and decisions, and to trust Him to always know what is best. Ask Him for the strength you need to not give up when you are sad, scared, or mad.

23

THIS IS NOT THE SEASON TO SOW SEEDS

> *How can a young man keep his way pure? By guarding it according to your word.*
>
> — *PSALM 119:9 ESV*

So, where are you at when it comes to girls? Do you have a girlfriend? What's the first thing you notice about a girl?

These are a few of the questions a group of teenage guys were asked at a church camp a few years ago. They were sitting in a guys only class talking about how to do the dating thing without compromising their purity and their relationship with God. Here are some of the answers they gave:

*I want to date, but honestly, there's no one at our school I want to date. If they are nice enough to date, they already have a boyfriend. The rest of the girls, which is most of them, flirt and practically dare you to say no to having sex with them.

-Anthony age 17

*I had a girlfriend. She's a nice girl in every way, but she wears so much makeup she ruined two of my shirts by putting her head on my shoulder: once at the movie and once at a school dance. And she's so weird about not eating junk and not getting sweaty or messing up her hair. She's boring, so I just told her I just wanted to be friends.

-Tommy aged 16

*Living in a small town makes it hard. The girls in my class are either related to me—four of them are my first cousins—or I've gone to school with them since kindergarten and I just don't like them like that. I'm not the only guy who feels that way, either. But we aren't blind, and we have hormones, so it makes it hard sometimes not to go online and find websites we shouldn't be looking at.

-Seth age 15

*I have a girlfriend. She's a Christian, too. But you guys know that because she's here, too, and you've known her a long time just like I have. Just because we're Christians doesn't mean we don't have feelings and hormones, though, so we set some boundaries for ourselves, and we have some people we trust to hold us accountable. We also do our best to not get in situations where we might be tempted. Like, we are never alone at her house or mine. We don't go cruising around just for fun, and things like that.

-Forrest age 16

*My parents were both raised in Christian homes, and they've raised me and my sisters in a Christian home. They are good parents, but some of you know what happened with my oldest sister. So, after that, Mom and Dad decided to be a lot stricter with Cici and me. I get mad sometimes because it doesn't seem fair sometimes. They won't allow either of us to date until we are eighteen. We can "court", which means an adult must be in the same or next room. So, I'm not really on any girl's radar to go out with. I know my parents worry and all, but they don't realize that just because I can't date doesn't mean I don't think about girls and sex and all that. Not being able to have a girlfriend makes all that worse. It's like that whole thing about telling someone no, only makes them want it more.

-Judson age 14

Being curious about girls and sex and having all those thoughts and feelings isn't bad. God put them in your DNA when He created you and then said, "Very good!" These things are normal and will play major roles in your life when the time is right, i.e., when you get married.

CASE IN POINT

One of the most confusing things in the Bible is the way a lot of people in the Old Testament had more than one wife, Jacob and David for example. But you don't have to go very deep into their lives to see what a mess their lives were because of having more than one wife. It doesn't make any sense to us, especially since a lot of the laws God gave Moses are about the sins a man and woman can get caught up in when they aren't totally committed to each other. Or the sins that happen when guys and girls have sex outside of marriage. But God allowed it to happen for a reason, and we know that He never makes mistakes. So….

By the time Jesus was born and the books of the New Testament were written, things had changed. One husband for one wife…the end. The New Testament also talks a lot about being pure and resisting the temptation of sexual sins.

USE IT FOR YOU

1: What boundaries or rules have your parents set for you about girls and dating? Or have they? If so, what are they and what do you think about them?

2: Be honest—how hard is it for you to resist porn sites, getting too physical with a girl, and watching movies that are not in line with Christian beliefs?

3: Do you think the Bible's expectations and rules about sex and purity are old fashioned and unrealistic? Why or why not?

4: Do you talk, look at, and treat girls the way you would want a boy to talk, look at, and treat your sister? Don't just answer "yes" or "no". Take the time to write down your thoughts and feelings about this.

24

THAT'S A SIN????

So whoever knows the right thing to do and fails to do it, for him it is sin.

— *JAMES 4:17 ESV*

It took less than a day for nine-year-old Fred to make a new friend when he and his family moved to their new house. The family that lived next to them had four kids. One of them was also a nine-year-old boy, Jonah. Jonah and his family were great neighbors. So, when Jonah asked Fred to go to Vacation Bible School with him, Fred's mom said yes.

Fred had never been to a church. His parents said they didn't have time and didn't think it was all that important. After the first day, Fred wasn't sure how important church was, but he sure did have a good time, so when Jonah asked him to go with him again the next day, and the day after that, Fred gladly agreed.

During the lesson on that third day, the teacher started talking about something called sin. Fred wasn't sure what that was, but it sounded a little sad and...and scary. He tried to figure it out by himself, but curiosity got the best of him, so while they were doing a craft project, he asked the teacher, "What is sin?"

The teacher wanted to make sure she understood Fred's question, so she asked him if he wanted to know *if* something in particular was a sin—like stealing and beating someone up—or *what* it means to sin. Fred said he wanted to know what sin is. "What's the meaning of the word *sin*?" he asked.

The teacher had never been asked that question before. She assumed (like most people who go to church, do) that everyone knows what sin is. But since that wasn't the case, she opened her Bible to the verse in James you read at the top of the page. After that she started listing some things God tells us are sins. She finished by telling Fred that she was going to give him something special the next day, a Bible of his very own. Then he could start reading and learning for himself. She added, "whenever you have any questions or don't understand something, you can always ask me or Jonah's mom or dad. We will help you understand, so that you can learn as much as you want about how fantastic and wonderful God is."

CASE IN POINT

One of the most powerful accounts in the Bible is in Acts, chapter eight. The disciples and other believers were being beaten and persecuted because of their faith. By the government and by the Jewish leaders who refused to believe that Jesus was the Messiah. FYI: Saul, who later became Paul, was one of the biggest persecutors of them all.

Anyway, Philip, one of the disciples, left Jerusalem to preach in Samaria. Lots of people were baptized into Jesus while he was there, so God sent an angel to tell Philip to go to Gaza so he could tell the people there about Jesus and that's what he did. But while he was walking from Samaria to Gaza, he saw a high-ranking soldier from Ethiopia (called a eunuch) sitting alongside the road in his chariot, reading what the prophet Isaiah had written. When Philip asked him what he was doing, the eunuch told him, but said he didn't really understand it. Who was this Savior and Messiah Isaiah was talking about?

Philip didn't waste any time telling the eunuch everything about Jesus: how He was born, about His ministry, His death, His resurrection, and that He had gone back to heaven. Philip finished by telling the eunuch how he could become a Christian, by telling him what Jesus said just before he went back to heaven and like Peter did back in Acts 2.

Then Jesus came to them and said, "All authority in heaven and on earth has been given to me. Therefore go and make disciples of all nations, baptizing them in the name of the Father and of the Son and of the Holy

Spirit, and teaching them to obey everything I have commanded you. And surely I am with you always, to the very end of the age."

— *MATTHEW 28:18–20 NIV*

> *When the people heard this, they were cut to the heart and said to Peter and the other apostles, "Brothers, what shall we do?" Peter replied, "Repent and be baptized, every one of you, in the name of Jesus Christ for the forgiveness of your sins. And you will receive the gift of the Holy Spirit.*

— *ACTS 2:37–38 NIV*

As soon as Philip said this, the eunuch pointed to a nearby pond or lake and said (I'm going to paraphrase) "There's some water, so what are we waiting for? I want to be baptized now." So, Philip baptized the Ethiopian eunuch. Immediately after that, an angel took Philip, and it is unlikely that the two men ever saw each other again.

Now, let's spend a minute or two talking about why this event speaks so powerfully about understanding what sin is and what it is not.

*The eunuch didn't understand everything Isaiah wrote, but he recognized that it was written with authority and that it was true.

*The eunuch understood the importance of being on "Team Jesus".

*The eunuch also understood that in order to be on "Team Jesus" he had to submit to the authority of the One in charge, God. So, even though he still had lots to learn and questions to be answered, the eunuch knew that anything we do or say that contradicts God is sin, and that the best way to distance himself from sin, was to get as close to God as possible by obeying Him in all things.

USE IT FOR YOU

1: What is your definition of sin?

2: Which sins do you struggle with the most, and why?

3: Are there things God calls sin that you think shouldn't be? If so, what are they, and why?

4: Have you ever asked or told a friend or family member that something they did (or are doing) is a sin? If so, how did they respond?

5: What are some things you can do to speak out against sin in your school and your community? Will you?

MORE FROM THE BIBLE

Look up the following verses. Read each one and think about what it is saying to YOU.

- Romans 3:23
- Romans 6:23
- 1 Corinthians 6:9–10
- 1 John 1:9

PRAYER PROMPT

Pray for courage to say no to the sins the devil tempts you with. Pray for courage to not accept sin as something good or normal. Pray for courage to offer others advice and encouragement to avoid sin.

25

I'M JUST NOT SURE

> *He who did not spare his own Son, but gave him up for us all—how will he not also, along with him, graciously give us all things?*
>
> — *ROMANS 8:32*

When Joel was nine, he saw a commercial on television for a hovercraft toy that looked amazing. So, when his grandma asked him what he wanted for Christmas, that hovercraft was at the top of the list. On Christmas Eve, Joel was thrilled when he opened his gift. Grandma and Grandpa did not disappoint.

The hovercraft was a whole other story. It was a huge disappointment. It was nothing like the one in the television commercial. Joel was sad and mad. He felt bad that his grandparents had wasted money on a piece of junk toy. When he told his parents, they said they were sorry because they knew how excited he had been about it. But they also told him he should learn something important from it—that when something looks too good to be true, it usually is.

Have you ever thought that about God? Have you ever wondered if all the stuff about God's love and forgiveness is too good to be true? Or maybe you've even wondered if all those miracles you've heard and read in the Bible are true—that there is no possible way a guy could have been swallowed by a fish... and lived to talk about it. Or that all a guy had to do was raise his arms over his head and an entire body of water would separate long enough for thousands and thousands of people could cross over without getting mud on their sandals. And why should you think that all Jesus had to do was pray and a few pieces of bread and a couple of fish turned into enough to feed thousands? That people were healed just because Jesus said a few words?

If your answer to any or all these questions is "yes", don't feel bad. Everyone has asked those very questions. It's a lot to wrap your head around. You need to understand, though, that no matter how much you doubt or how many questions you have, the answer is always, ALWAYS going to be the same. The answer is "yes". Every single word in the Bible is true. Always has been. Always will be. But at the end of the day, it is up to you to decide what you do with the truth.

FYI: **Choosing to believe is called FAITH.**

CASE IN POINT

Luke 9:17–25 is a perfect example of what we are talking about. Jesus was teaching a large group of people and healing several who came to him asking for help. One man asked Jesus to help his son. The boy was possessed by a demon. We'll talk more about what this means another day, but for now, you need to know that the boy would have seizures and lose control of himself. He would throw himself down on the ground and even into the fires they used for cooking and staying warm. The man (and probably his wife, too) were out of ideas on how to keep the boy safe. So, when he heard that Jesus was in town, he decided to see if everything he had heard about Jesus was true.

When he finally made his way through the crowd and stood face to face with Jesus, he said, "If you can do anything to help him, please do it."

Jesus' response gives you the impression that Jesus was a little hurt or maybe even a bit sad because of the man's doubts. "If" he could help the boy?! Of course, he could help!!

USE IT FOR YOU

If you are like a lot of people, some of your ideas about what God is like are wrong. If you only see God as a superhero who doesn't feel emotion because He is God, and because He is too busy being powerful and holy and is so busy keeping the earth on its axis, the universe in place, *and* listening to everyone's prayers, you aren't seeing God for who he really is. You aren't giving God credit for knowing and understanding how you feel and what you are thinking...or for having doubts. So, come on, give God a chance.

1: Read Genesis 6:5–8 and write three or four sentences describing how this affects your thoughts and feelings about God's personality.

2: When you have problems, questions, or doubts about the following, who do you go to for help and advice?

- Math
- Girls
- Peer pressure into doing something you're not comfortable with
- How to complete a chore or an assignment
- Disagreements with friends or family
- What to do about college

3: Why did you go to those people?

4: What doubts and questions do you have about the Bible and about God or Jesus?

5: Who and where do you think is the best person (or people) and place to go for answers you can depend on to be true and right?

MORE FROM THE BIBLE

Look up the following verses. Read each one and think about what it is saying to YOU.

- Isaiah 40:28
- Hebrews 11:1
- Jeremiah 17:7–8

PRAYER PROMPT

Ask God to give you people you can trust to help you when you have questions and doubts. Ask Him to help you understand the Bible, and to make your heart and mind open and willing to learn, trust, and obey.

26

EATING AND EXERCISE—GOD HIGHLY RECOMMENDS IT

> *Pay careful attention to yourselves and to all the flock, in which the Holy Spirit has made you overseers, to care for the church of God which he obtained with his own blood.*
>
> — *ACTS 20:28 ESV*

Back before you were born, a movie called *The Rookie* hit the big screen. It is about a small-town high school teacher who is also the baseball coach who thought he missed his chance to play professional baseball. He agrees to try out again *only if* his team has a winning season. He finds himself trying out for the minor leagues and throwing pitches at 95mph.

Fact number one: the team didn't have a winning season and the coach didn't just wake up one morning throwing that fast and accurately, I might add. It took hours, days, and weeks of dedication, discipline, and practice for them to achieve these levels of excellence.

Fact number two: all that discipline and dedication didn't begin and end on the baseball field. It was part of everything they did. Their schoolwork, what they did in their spare time, who they spent time with, how much rest they got, what they ate…everything.

Fact number three: *The Rookie* is a great movie. You should watch it.

The verse at the beginning of this chapter is talking about watching out for each other and keeping each other on the right track when it comes to being a Christian. But when you stop and think about it, doesn't that (or shouldn't that) include how we take care of our bodies? After all, if we aren't in good physical condition, we can't do the things God needs and expects us to do. You also need to remember that when you disrespect your body this way, you are disrespecting God because you are His creation.

CASE IN POINT

Back in Genesis, chapter one, God told Adam and Eve He had created all sorts of good things for them to eat, including every plant and tree that had seeds in it. Depending on the plant, they could eat either the fruits or veggies it produced or the leaves and stems. No fish. No meat. Just fruits, veggies, and grains. That's what He gave them to eat ***because*** He knew those were the things that would best feed and fuel their bodies.

Now let's jump forward a few chapters in Genesis. In chapter nine, God gives the "all clear" for Noah and his family, along with all their critters, to (finally) get off the ark. It is at that point that God changed the way people eat. God added fish, birds, and mammals (meat) to the menu. We aren't given any reasons for the change. It might have been because most plants and trees need time to grow before they produce food, and God knew Noah and his family couldn't wait that long to eat (who could, right?!). So, once again God gave people what He knew they needed to feed and fuel their bodies.

God also knew Noah and his family, along with the rest of us (including you), needed to move and use our bodies, which is why our bodies *need daily* exercise. Exercise makes our bodies work the way they should. So, if you think emptying the dishwasher is asking too much, try having to *make* your dishes out of wood, strips of bark, or rocks. You might also want to think twice about complaining about having to fold and put your laundry away, until you hunt, kill, skin, and tan the hide of a deer or soak thin sheets of bark in water so you can shape it into a rain poncho.

USE IT FOR YOU

1: How much time do you spend playing sports, running, walking, and doing chores?

2: Do you eat fruits and vegetables? Which ones are your favorites?

3: How many times a week do you eat junk food, fast food, or something that comes in a box, bag, or can?

4: Make a list of activities you will do that will help you get more exercise.

5: Make a list of unhealthy foods you eat. Next to each one, list a healthy food you can and will eat instead.

6: Talk to your mom and dad about making healthier food choices and getting more exercise. Ask them if they will help you make this a family project.

MORE FROM THE BIBLE

Look up the following verses. Read each one and think about what it is saying to YOU.

- 1 Corinthians 10:31
- Daniel 1:12–16
- 1 Corinthians 3:17

PRAYER PROMPT

Ask God to help you make good choices when it comes to what you eat and the way you spend your spare time. Thank God for your healthy body, ask Him to forgive you for not feeding and fueling your body the way you should, and ask Him to give you the right attitude for hard work and doing your chores.

27

YOUR PARENTS ARE NOT THE ENEMY

> *"Honor your father and your mother, that your days may be long in the land that the Lord your God is giving you.*
>
> — *EXODUS 20:12 ESV*

Are you a professional eye roller? Did you get to that level by rolling your eyes at almost everything your parents say to you?

How long has it been since you said, "You don't understand!" Or "You wouldn't understand." Or "You don't have a clue about what I'm going through."? Was it this morning before you left for school? Last night? Last week? A month ago? And why did you say it?

At what age did you stop believing your parents were your best and most reliable source for good advice and information?

How often do you ignore your parents, especially when they tell you to do something (or not do something)? How often do you accuse them of treating you like a child? Not trusting you? Not respecting you?

If you are squirming in your seat or talking to the book trying to justify your attitude, you can stop. It's safe to say just about every kid on Earth is guilty of doing some of these things. Besides, God is the only one who can hear and see you, and He already knows.

Oh, and one more thing...there is nothing you can say to make it okay to say and do those things. Why? Because...

- They are your parents. They are responsible for you. They are in authority over you. It's their job to teach, guide, monitor, decide what you are and aren't ready for, and to discipline you. And most importantly, they love you.
- Your parents DO understand. The details of the situations they faced when they were your age aren't the same, but *they have been where you are now.* They have been kids. They have been teenagers. And for the record, it hasn't been all that long ago. You, however, have never been an adult, which means you may be the one who doesn't understand.

Ouch! That hurts a little bit, doesn't it? But what's that they say about 'no pain, no gain'? I don't mean to be rude, hurtful, or to diss your feelings. Not at all. But this is one of those things that falls under the category of "for your own good".

Yikes! How's that for another bucket of cold water in your face? Sorry, but you need to know...to really know that your parents are not the enemy. They really do love you. They just want what is best for you. They want you to have the best life and be your best self. Are they going to make mistakes? You bet! Are they always right? No, but then, neither is anyone else. You can be sure that even when they do make mistakes, and even when they don't get it right, it's never on purpose and they aren't trying to spoil all your fun and ruin your life. Just sayin'.

CASE IN POINT

One of David's sons—Absalom—was a bit of a rebel. In 2 Samuel 18:33, David tried his best to keep Absolom from messing up, but the guy just wouldn't listen. He died young and it was all because he wouldn't listen to his dad.

Let's look at 1 Samuel 2:34: Old Eli, the priest who raised Samuel, had two sons of his own. Their names were Phineas and Hophni. Both these boys grew up to be men who thought they could do whatever they wanted because their dad was the high priest. They took advantage of Eli's position and reputation, by breaking rules and treating people badly. They also ended up getting killed because of their behavior and disrespect for God and for their dad.

And finally, let's look at the infamous prodigal son. In Luke 15:11–32, he was the son in Jesus' parable who asked his dad for his inheritance money...before the dad died. Even though the dad had to know it wasn't a good idea, he gave the son the money. Even though the Bible doesn't come right out and say it, I think part of the reason the dad gave it to him, was to teach the son a few lessons. Lessons, like why it's not a good idea to waste money, why being a party animal always ends badly, and that your parents really are smarter and wiser than kids think they are, and that they love you more than you can imagine.

Anyway, the son took the money and ran. Literally. He ran away to the big city, wasted it all, and ended up living in a pigpen without any friends or food. No one wanted anything to do with him once his money was all gone. Except good ole' Dad.

When the son realized what a mess he had made of his life, he swallowed his pride and went home. He apologized for being such a jerk and asked his dad for a job. The dad was so happy to see his son, he forgave him for the mistakes he had made and welcomed him back to the family.

Jesus told this parable to teach us that God's love for us is so big and so deep and so strong that He will forgive us for anything when we ask AND when we repent (change our attitude and actions).

Your parents will, too.

USE IT FOR YOU

1: How often do you argue with your parents?

2: What are most of the arguments about?

3: If you disagree with the rules and guidelines your parents set for you, do you complain about it? Ignore them and hope you don't get caught? Or do you have a respectful discussion about why you disagree and try to either understand their side of things or come up with a solution you are both happy with?

4: Which rules and expectations do your parents have for you that you think are unfair? List them below. Next to each one, write what you think it should be. Show the list to your parents and ask them to discuss it with you.

5: Think about those times when your parents have been there for you—for anything and everything. Will you take the time today to tell them how much you love them and appreciate them? Will you have an honest conversation with yourself about the things you should do to let them know how much you love and appreciate them?

MORE FROM THE BIBLE

Look up the following verses. Read each one and think about what it is saying to YOU.

- Proverbs 29:15
- Proverbs 1:8–9
- Colossians 3:20
- Hebrews 12:11

PRAYER PROMPT

Thank God for giving you parents who love you. Ask God to help you be more respectful, helpful, loving, and kind to your parents.

28

BUT WHAT IF THEY AREN'T THAT KIND OF PARENTS

> *For my father and my mother have forsaken me, but the Lord will take me in.*
>
> — *PSALM 27:10 ESV*

Remember a few chapters back when we talked about Charles and the fact that he grew up with parents who were abusive? That's a rotten situation for a kid to be in, especially since none of us asks to be born. But we all know things are not always the way they are supposed to be. Sometimes we cannot control what happens—even though we do everything right or when we do our best to keep it from happening.

That means you or someone you know may be in the same situation Charles was in. I'm sorry about that. Nothing about that is right. And nothing any kid does makes it okay for parents to mistreat their kids. But I want you to know that YOU ARE

NOT ALONE. God is watching out for you, and He will protect you. I also want you to know that when you ask God to send you people to love you, watch over you, and help you grow up to be a man who loves people the right way, He will. He will send those people to you.

CASE IN POINT

King Saul was the kind of man who was so worried about being powerful and popular, that he didn't know how to love his kids the way he should. He was crazy jealous of anyone who got more attention than he did, especially David. David got lots of attention because he was a brave soldier, he was humble and nice, and he honored God. His best friend also happened to be Jonathan, one of King Saul's sons.

When David told his best friend Jonathan that his dad, King Saul, was trying to kill him in 1 Samuel 20:1, Jonathan didn't believe it. It couldn't be true! Johnathan knew how loyal David was to King Saul. David didn't argue with his friend. Instead, he came up with a plan to prove he was right. It was sort of a code phrase kind of thing. He told Jonathan to ask his dad something. If his dad answered one way, then Jonathan was right, and David was wrong. But if King Saul answered another way, then David was right, and Jonathan was wrong.

Long story short, David was right and Jonathan had to face the fact that this dad had been lying to him and scheming behind his back to kill his best friend. This was definitely not a warm and fuzzy father-son moment.

Another father-son (and mom) moment in the Bible that isn't all that stellar involves Isaac and his son, Esau. In Genesis 27:5–10, Isaac's wife, Rebecca, along with Esau's twin brother, Jacob, tricked Isaac into giving everything to Jacob that should have gone to Esau. When the plot is uncovered and Isaac and Esau realized what had happened, Esau begged his dad to undo the wrong and hold Rebecca and Jacob accountable for their actions. Isaac didn't do it. He said it was a matter of being duty-bound. That he couldn't go back on his word. That had to be rough on Esau.

The third Bible account between a father and son (and mother, again, too) is found in the New Testament. In John 9:1–25, Jesus healed a blind man. The man had been born blind. After Jesus healed him, the Jewish leaders started asking questions about "this Jesus character." They were jealous of Him, threatened by His power, and wanted to get rid of Him. So, the Jewish leaders called in the guy's parents and asked them what they thought. You would think they would be thrilled that their son could now see for the first time in his life. Instead, they threw him under the bus! They told the Jewish leaders that they didn't know anything about the situation, that their son is an adult, and they don't want to get involved. Ouch!

No matter what your situation is at home—even if you have parents who aren't in your corner—you have a Father who loves you more than you can imagine. He is also a parent who can and will protect you and make sure you have everything you need. He is God.

USE IT FOR YOU

1: What is your definition of an abusive or neglectful parent?

2: Are you and your parents getting along? Are they physically or emotionally abusive? Do you argue or fight because they don't share your faith in God? Are you disobedient and disrespectful? Do you argue and fight because you don't share their faith? Take the time to think about the reasons you have a difficult relationship with them. Once you figure this out, you will be able to get the help you need.

3: Do you have at least two or three adults in your life you can trust? People who you can confide in, who you can go to for advice and help? Who are they? Go to them if you are being abused.

4. Do you personally know someone that is suffering from abuse or being neglected? What resources can you provide to help this person? Could you give them the phone number of your youth leader at church or invite them to join you? Could you tell one of the adults you just mentioned above? Maybe you could share or gift them this devotional?

MORE FROM THE BIBLE

Look up the following verses. Read each one and think about what it is saying to YOU.

- Ephesians 6:4
- Colossians 3:21
- Psalm 34:18
- Psalm 147:3

PRAYER PROMPT

Ask God to keep you safe, to give you someone to trust, and ask Him to send someone to help your parents. Pray that your parents will get to know Jesus and that they will accept Him as their Lord and Savior.

29

POST IT...RECORD IT...SHARE IT... UPLOAD IT...SEND IT...REPEAT

> *I will not set before my eyes anything that is worthless. I hate the work of those who fall away; it shall not cling to me. A perverse heart shall be far from me; I will know nothing of evil.*
>
> — PSALM 101:3–4 ESV

If you are like most guys your age, TikTok, Snapchat, and YouTube are your primary picks when it comes to social media. Oh, and Reddit. I almost forgot about that one. Instagram is still a thing for some of you, too, but Twitter and Facebook...not so much, right? Vine? What even is that?

Social media is like anything else—it has its good points and bad. Social media lets you stay connected with people you don't see very often. It's a good way to communicate changes in practice times, post scores, and it even lets you share pictures with grandparents who can't be there for all those special events. But social media is also the place where shaming and bullying happens, where gossip and lies are spread, where sex trafficking and porn happens, and people's lives are permanently wrecked or destroyed by someone's careless, thoughtless words or pictures.

If you allow social media to steal your time away from your family, if it prevents you from being fully present in your conversations, or takes precedence over homework, you might be falling into the idolatry trap. If this is you, no judgement here. It's easy to do but it needs to be addressed and fixed. Try setting hard stops on the time limits for each app. When the alarm goes off respect yourself enough to listen to it.

When it comes to understanding the long-term effects and consequences it has, you've got a lot of learning left to do. You can clean your cookies, wipe your hard drives, and delete all the files you want to, but once something is out there, it's out there. It's not going away. Someone, somewhere, somehow, someplace keeps it stored for whoever, whenever, however, and for whatever reason they might want it. Some of you (hopefully most of you) are thinking this isn't about you. In fact, you hope the videos you put out there on how to get to the next level of whatever game you are playing, your crazy-fun bike ramp escapades, the goofy tricks your dog does, and the way you slammed down six pieces of pizza in less time than anyone else, go VIRAL!!!!!! If that's the case, then yes! Go for it!

But...

But if you are one of the guys out there who are spreading rumors, shame on you and STOP! If you are bullying someone, trash-talking a teacher, coach, your parents, or anyone...STOP! If you are guilty of asking for pictures you shouldn't be looking at, searching for pictures you shouldn't be looking at, spreading hate, fueling the fights, or anything else that puts a frown on God's face, STOP! In the end this only crushes your confidence and spirit. It's not cool.

Let's be real. Social Media is not going anywhere. The apps may change popularity but some form of it is here to stay. Let's make it our mission to use it for good and for God's Glory. A great leader knows how to encourage his peers. Your job...the things God has commanded you to do, is forgive, turn the other cheek, and to love and treat other people (that means everyone) the way you want them to treat you. Use your platforms to uplift peoples' spirits, inspire others, and show mercy. Infuse your posts with the Word and watch your confidence sore! One of best ways you can lead is in the palm of your hands. Use it for good.

So...

Stop and ask yourself these two questions: Would I do this if Jesus was looking over my shoulder?" And if the answer is "no", ask yourself, "What would Jesus do, instead?"

Then do it! Do what Jesus would do every time.

CASE IN POINT

Social media and the internet were obviously not things neither Jesus nor the early Christians had to deal with. Your grandparents, and even some of your parents didn't have to deal with it until they were in their teens or adults. But that doesn't mean they weren't tempted to say or do some of the same things you are, but in person instead of from behind a screen. Whether in person or online, the problem is still the same.

Jesus' disciples were ordinary guys who were living ordinary lives when Jesus said, "Hey, come with me." They weren't straight-A students. They weren't rich or famous. They were just plain, ordinary people. Matthew was even a bit of a lawbreaker. His job as a tax collector almost guaranteed that he bullied people into paying more taxes than they owed. Yet Jesus saw something in all of them. We call it potential. He knew they had the potential to be leaders, preachers, teachers, elders, husbands, fathers, and friends, who would bring other people to know Jesus the way they did.

Jesus also knew that they were not perfect. He knew that they would get angry, get into arguments, get discouraged, have doubts about what they were doing, wish they didn't ever have to wonder where and what they would eat or if someone would offer them a place to stay. He knew they would feel scared at times and get tired of always having to defend themselves to the Jewish leaders and stay one step ahead of them so they wouldn't end up in jail (or worse).

Jesus knew these things about the disciples, but He still chose them. He chose them *and* He equipped them for the jobs He needed them to do. One of the ways He did this was to make sure they understood *how they were supposed to respond to people who treated them badly.*

Jesus said...

- Matthew 18:20–21 Then Peter came up and said to him, "Lord, how often will my brother sin against me, and I forgive him? As many as seven times?" Jesus said to him, "I do not say to you seven times, but seventy-seven times.
- Matthew 12:36 I tell you, on the day of judgment people will give account for every careless word they speak.
- Luke 6:27 But I say to you who hear, love your enemies, do good to those who hate you....

USE IT FOR YOU

1: How much time do you spend on social media?

2: What type of activities do you participate in? Uploading videos? Chatting? Checking out other people? Shaming? Bullying? Posting inappropriate and negative content?

3: Have you ever been hurt by someone's actions toward you on social media? What happened and why? How did you respond?

4: Do you think social media is out of control? If so, how do you think you can solve this problem so that it doesn't influence you in the wrong way?

5: Social Media Challenge: I challenge you to do something nice for someone over social media. No, a simple like does not count. You could reach out to someone you have not talked to in a while, send someone a sincere compliment, or share a story that honors God.

6. Book Reviews are the biggest compliments and acts of kindness you can give to an author. If you have been enjoying this devotional, please take a moment to leave a review describing your experience here or scan the QR code. Your review has the potential to help thousands of young men just like you. Thank you.

MORE FROM THE BIBLE

Look up the following verses. Read each one and think about what it is saying to YOU.

- Psalm 101:5

- Exodus 20:16
- Titus 3:2

PRAYER PROMPT

Ask God to put a guard over your heart, mind, and hands when you use social media. Ask God to help you always remember to think about how your social media activity will affect others.

30

WHAT IS FAITH AND HOW CAN I GET SOME?

> *Now faith is the assurance of things hoped for, the conviction of things not seen.*
>
> — *HEBREWS 11:1 ESV*

There you go—that's what faith is. It is believing something is real and true and putting your trust in "it," without seeing proof of it first.

For example, you probably have a drawer in your kitchen where the knives, forks, and spoons are kept. You cannot see what's inside that drawer unless you open it, but you have total one-hundred-percent faith that when you do, that's what will be there. Not bowls. Not potholders, foil, or those baggies for snacks…just knives, forks, and spoons.

Faith is Like Chocolate, which is a devotional book for people your age, also does a great job in explaining what faith is. Take a look…

"You probably don't remember the first time you tasted chocolate, do you? The first piece of chocolate to touch your lips probably came from your grandma, your Sunday school teacher, or the nice lady at the bank.

Where you got it isn't really all that important, though. Why you ate it...that's what matters.

Think about it…chocolate isn't the prettiest thing to look at. It's a little slab of brown stuff with lines and words on it, or a small cylinder-shaped piece of brown goo. You know, when you take the time to stop to think about it, chocolate doesn't look very appetizing, does it? So why did you eat it? You ate it because you trusted the person who gave it to you. When they told you how good it would be, you believed them. But what happened after that? What happened after you took that first bite? You did take another bite, didn't you?

Of course, you did! The question, though, is why? Why did you take the next bite…and the next (and the countless ones after that)? You kept eating because the first bite was everything you were told it would be, so you expected each bite afterwards to be the same.

Do you see what happened? After that first bite, instead of trusting the person who gave you the chocolate, your faith was transferred from the person who gave it to you to the chocolate…

Faith in God is a lot like eating chocolate. The first time you trusted God (put your faith in Him), it was most likely because someone told you to.

Your parents or youth leaders or the preacher at your church told you it was the thing to do. They told you faith was real and expected you to trust that what they said was true. You trust these people. You know they love you and want what's best for you, so you do it. You ask God to do something for you.

I'm not talking about something selfish or 'out there.' I'm talking about something like helping you through a scary or tough situation. Or maybe something like giving you the courage to break a bad habit or resist the temptation to do something you know you shouldn't.

Or maybe you were reading your Bible and decided to take verses like Psalm 37:5–6 and Mark 11:22–24 out for a spin. And found out for yourself, it really works! God is there for you! You trusted Him and He was there!

That's real faith. Once you realized God can be trusted and that He never breaks His promises, your faith was no longer in the person who told you to have faith in God, but in God himself."

**Excerpt used by permission from the author. "Faith is Like Chocolate" (published 2018)*

See how faith works?

CASE IN POINT

All throughout the Gospels of Matthew, Mark, Luke, and John, we read about people coming to Jesus asking Him to heal them or to heal a friend or member of their family. These people didn't wake up one morning and decide to find some random guy they thought *might* be able to help them. No, that wasn't it, at all. They came to Jesus because they either heard what He had done for other people or had witnessed a miracle or two with their own eyes. That's not a bad thing. Not at all! But it's not what Bible teachers and preachers would call "blind faith."

Jesus didn't mind, because He knew that the people He taught, helped, and healed, would tell everyone what had happened. That's "word of mouth" and it's a powerful thing. Those people would tell their friends and family, who would then tell theirs, and so on. And when those people—the ones who didn't see or experience Jesus firsthand—chose to believe, obey, and follow Jesus, THEY were making that choice out of FAITH.

Jesus knew the day was coming (sooner instead of later) when faith would be what brought people to Him—to accept His gift of salvation and a home in Heaven. He talked about it after He came back to life that Sunday morning (Easter Sunday). Here's how it went...

Now Thomas (also known as Didymus one of the Twelve, was not with the disciples when Jesus came. So, the other disciples told him, "We have seen the Lord! But he said to them, "Unless I see the nail marks in his hands and put my finger where the nails were, and put my hand into his side, I will not believe." A week later his disciples were in the house again, and Thomas was with them. Though the doors were locked, Jesus came and stood among them and said, "Peace be with you!" Then he said to Thomas, "Put your finger here; see my hands. Reach out your hand and put it into my side. Stop doubting and believe." Thomas said to him, "My Lord and my God!" Then Jesus told him, "Because you have seen me, you have believed; blessed are those who have not seen and yet have believed." ~John 20:24–29 NIV

Faith is what you need to make that same choice.

USE IT FOR YOU

1: Before you read today's definition, how would you have defined the word "faith"?

2: What would you say to someone who says faith is silly or even a sign of weakness or laziness?

3: When has it been hard for you to have faith in God? Why?

4: When and how has God rewarded your faith?

5: What do you think you need to do to grow your faith? Will you commit to doing that?

MORE FROM THE BIBLE

Look up the following verses. Read each one and think about what it is saying to YOU.

- Romans 10:17
- 2 Corinthians 5:7
- James 1:6
- 1 Timothy 4:12

PRAYER PROMPT

Ask God to give you a stronger faith. Tell God you love Him, believe Him, believe in Him, and want to grow to put Him in charge of your whole life.

31

ROLL DOGS FOR LIFE

Iron sharpens iron, and one man sharpens another.

— *PROVERBS 27:17 ESV*

What do you know about the Paqui One Chip Challenge?

Okay, so that was a dumb question. You know all about it, don't you? Or at least you think you do.

Did you know the challenge is dangerous (among other things)? Did you know kids and young adults who are foolish enough to try it often end up in the ER? Did you know the shock of something that hot and spicy causes your heart to race, your blood pressure to spike rapidly, and your stomach to revolt? Which means you are gonna puke your guts out. Did you know the chip is so hot that it can leave "burn" scars on your tongue, mouth, tastebuds, and your throat?

And finally, did you know that anyone who would challenge, dare, bully, or entice you to take this challenge is NOT a good friend?

FYI: If you don't believe these things are true—that it can't be all that bad—look it up. Several teenagers in California who took the challenge together made the news because they all went to the ER together. Another twenty-two-year-old college student in Missouri spent a couple of days in the hospital because he had such a serious adverse reaction.

Parents, teachers, and other adults who work with kids are shaking their heads, wondering why anyone would even make something like that. What's the point? Why would you want to make something that you know is going to hurt people? It doesn't make any sense!

Anyway...people who claim to be your friends, but who say or do things that hurt you (physically, emotionally, or spiritually) are not your friends. Friends don't do things like that. Friends sharpen you—help you be a better person. Real friends want you to succeed, they don't ask you or try to bully you into disobeying your parents or do things you know God is not okay with. So, when you are choosing who your *friends* are—who you are going to hang out with, who you will trust to accept and respect your values and faith—choose wisely. Choose guys who keep you sharp.

CASE IN POINT

In the eighth chapter of the book of Acts, Peter and some of the other disciples went to Samaria and preached the Gospel to the

Samaritans. That was a bold thing for them to do, since the Jewish people and the Samaritans couldn't stand to be in the same room. They wouldn't even walk on the same side of the road or live in the same town with each other! But Peter and some of the others went because the Holy Spirit led them there.

Anyway...a lot of people came to hear what they had to say. Not only that, but they believed and were baptized into Jesus—just like Jesus told the disciples to do before He went back to Heaven. One of the guys who was baptized was a guy by the name of Simon.

Simon was a magician and was very popular with the people in Samaria. The Bible tells us that Simon believed what Peter taught, but what happens next proves that it's not enough to believe. Just like it's not enough for someone to say they are your friend. Simon wanted to pay the disciples money for "healing lessons and power." He offered to pay them to teach him how to do what they were doing—what God had given them the power to do.

The disciples didn't take Simon up on his offer. They knew immediately that he was NOT the kind of guy they should hang out with and not the kind of guy who should be trying to teach people to love and obey God. So, they told him to go away and get his act together. They told him he needed to repent, which meant he had to acknowledge past sins, stop sinning on purpose, ask God to forgive him for all the things he had done wrong, and to start obeying everything God commands and expects from those who claim to be part of His family.

USE IT FOR YOU

1: Who are your best friends—the people you spend most of your time with?

2: Are they Christians? Do they know you are a Christian?

3: Have you ever done anything you knew you shouldn't because a "friend" asked, dared, or told you to? What did you do? Why did you cave in? What happened?

4: Have you ever been that "friend"—the one who talked someone into doing something they shouldn't? If so, why?

5:

a) Write five or six words you believe describe what a true friend is.

b) Do you represent these qualities?

6: If you have close friends, friends you hang out with, who aren't a positive influence on you and who don't respect your values, we call these toxic relationships. You should highly consider exiting them out of your life. If you have friends like this, what are you going to do about it?

MORE FROM THE BIBLE

Look up the following verses. Read each one and think about what it is saying to YOU.

- 1 Corinthians 15:33
- Proverbs 13:20
- Proverbs 12:26

PRAYER PROMPT

Pray for wisdom in choosing your friends. Pray for strength to stand strong in the Lord against peer pressure. Pray for wisdom to be the right kind of friend. Ask God to bless you with good, true, Godly friends.

32

THE PRESSURE IS REAL

I will instruct you and teach you in the way you should go; I will counsel you with my eye upon you.

— *PSALM 32:8*

John and a few of his friends were sitting together on the bleachers in the high school gym, pretending to listen to a student and parent orientation meeting. The boys were about to be freshmen. If they were being honest, they were almost as nervous as they were excited. Coming into a new building that was a lot bigger than the middle school and junior high buildings was a little intimidating. They also knew that being the new kids on the block, so to speak, and having to prove themselves in football, soccer, tennis, golf, band, and practically everything else in school, wasn't going to be all that fun.

The boys sat up a little straighter and started listening more intently when John's mom asked a question. "Are you telling us we need to tell our kids they need to decide which career path they want to follow...now? And are you saying that the way they make out their schedule for high school—even this first year—will make or break their chances of reaching those goals?"

When the counselor nodded and said yes, John's mom spoke up again, "I am unapologetically and respectfully disagreeing with you. I've sat through four of these freshmen orientation meetings over the years with my other children and this is the first time I've heard this. I will also say that our older children, except for one, left high school supposedly knowing exactly which route they were taking but ended up going a completely different direction. Yet all four of them are happy, well-adjusted, and the three who are out of school, are self-supporting and thriving."

John and his friends weren't sure what to think at first, but when his mom stopped talking, almost every other parent in the room started clapping and saying things like, "She's right," "I agree," and "That's too much pressure on a kid that age."

John's mom and the other parents are right. Trying to get you to make such a big and important decision as that, without having everything you need to make it wisely, is wrong. It is wrong and it is a recipe for disaster. Failure, even.

Big decisions are best made by finding out what your options are, taking the time to weigh the options, and making the best choice(s) possible with the available knowledge that you currently have. Don't let peer pressure, guilt, trying to fit in or please anyone, push you into deciding too quickly or make the wrong choice.

CASE IN POINT

There are several situations in the Bible where people let peer pressure, guilt, trying to fit in, or trying to outsmart someone, lead to making poor choices and decisions. Sometimes they thought they were doing the right thing, but not always. Sometimes they knew they shouldn't do something, but they did it anyway.

- In 2 Samuel 24, even after God told David not to take a count of the men in his army, he did it anyway. Making that poor choice, led to him having to make another choice—a difficult choice. God told David he couldn't let his disobedience go unpunished, so He told David he had to choose between three punishments: three years of drought and famine (no rain or crops), three months of being attacked by their enemies, or three days of a deathly plague. David chose the three-day plague. It would be awful, but it would be shorter AND God would be the only one doing it. Their enemies wouldn't be involved. So, that's what God did, and in just under three days, over 70,000 Israelites died. All because David made a decision he shouldn't have made.
- Years before that happened, the Old Testament is filled with stories of King Saul, the first Israelite king, and his army fighting the Philistines. They were always fighting those guys. Anyway, things weren't going all that well,

which made Saul mad. Well, you know what can happen when you start spewing out words when you are angry. Sometimes you end up saying things you shouldn't. That's what Saul did. He made a decree (an announcement) that until they won the battle, no one was allowed to eat. Even when they came to a big old tree full of honey while they were making their way through the woods, they weren't allowed to even taste it. I know it doesn't make any sense to make soldiers go hungry, but that was where Saul's mind was at. There was just one little problem: Saul's son Jonathan was off fighting in another direction (and winning, by the way), but didn't hear the news about no food and ate some of it when he found it later that day.

FYI: Honey is a natural sugar source and gives your body energy and helps you think more clearly (no brain fog). So, after Jonathan ate a little of the honey, he was able to keep a clear head and push the Philistines back to their own land. When Saul found out what Jonathan had done —that he had disobeyed the no food rule—he was going to kill Jonathan! Even though Jonathan kept them from being beat down by the Philistines, King Saul was going to kill his own son over a little bit of honey and a rule Jonathan didn't even know about. Thankfully, the other soldiers spoke up and said they weren't going to let that happen. Jonathan's actions had saved them all and to kill him would be the worst thing he could possibly do.

- Pilate, the guy that handed down a sentence of crucifixion for Jesus, also made a tough decision based on peer pressure with a little bit of fear mixed in. He knew Jesus was innocent. In the four Gospels of Matthew, Mar, Luke, and John, Pilate tried to tell the Jewish mob of people screaming and yelling at him, that Jesus was innocent. He even tried to make a prisoner swap, but the Jewish people weren't having any of it. They wanted Jesus dead, and they didn't care what they had to do to make it happen. So, Pilate took the cowardly way out, handed Jesus over to them, and then tried to clear his conscience by saying he didn't want any part of what they did once he released him into their custody. He literally washed his hands of it! Pilate had more than enough facts to know he was making a mistake, but he let peer pressure, fear of being attacked and/or losing his job, and the chance to finally get in good with some of his superiors, take over.

FYI: The decision that Jesus had to die for our sins had been made looooooooooong before that, so even though Pilate made some bad decisions, ultimately, it was best for you, me, and everyone else who accepts Jesus as their Lord and Savior.

USE IT FOR YOU

1: When have you made decisions or choices without first getting all the facts? What happened?

2: Do you ever feel pressured or bullied to make choices and decisions you know you aren't ready to make? Give some examples.

3: Do you ever feel pressured or bullied to make choices and decisions you know you shouldn't make—to do things you know you shouldn't do? Why do you let this happen?

4: Who do you go to for help and advice when it comes to making decisions? Why do you trust them to help you?

5: How often do you use your Bible to help you make good and wise choices and decisions? If your answer is 'never' or 'not very often,' I encourage you to change that.

Did you know you can find EVERYTHING you need to know in the Bible? HINT: If you go to the website: www.openbible.info and go to the "Topical Bible" tab, you will find the alphabet at the top of the page. Click on the letter of the word or phrase you need help with. You will find verses to help you make the choices God wants you to make.

EXAMPLE: Letter F ❑ friends, family, faith, forgiveness, fear.

MORE FROM THE BIBLE

Look up the following verses. Read each one and think about what it is saying to YOU.

- James 1:5
- Philippians 4:6
- Proverbs 2:1–5

PRAYER PROMPT

Thank God for the Bible and all the wisdom and teachings in it. Ask God to help you always remember to go to the Bible for advice and information on how and when to make the best choices and decisions. Ask God to give you people you can trust to help you choose to be your best self all the time. Ask God to give you the ability to think before you speak and act.

33

THERE'S NO SHAME IN ASKING FOR HELP

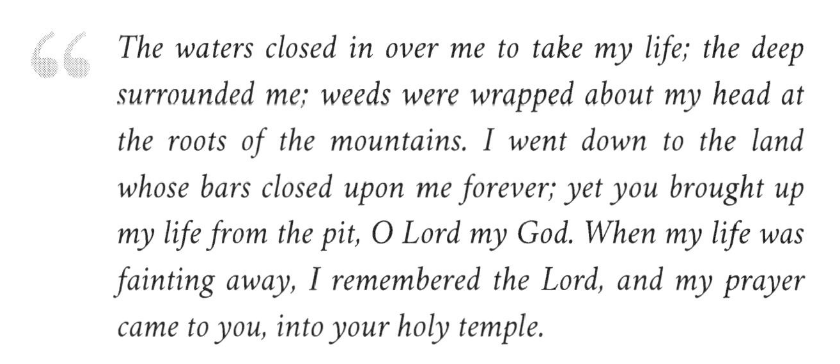

> *The waters closed in over me to take my life; the deep surrounded me; weeds were wrapped about my head at the roots of the mountains. I went down to the land whose bars closed upon me forever; yet you brought up my life from the pit, O Lord my God. When my life was fainting away, I remembered the Lord, and my prayer came to you, into your holy temple.*
>
> — *JONAH 2:5–7 ESV*

You aren't going to find words like "pretty" and "beautiful" in this book unless absolutely necessary to get the point across. This is one of those times, and the word is "beautiful" because there is no better word out there to describe what Jonah said. So, take a minute or two to read the verses at the top of the page again. And then again.

After you are done reading, think about a time when you or someone you know was in "over their head." Maybe you or your friend got caught cheating. Maybe you or your friend knew something *really* big about someone else but swore you wouldn't tell even though *not* telling could get them in big trouble or put them in danger.

Now ask yourself this question: When or if this happens to you, what are you going to do and who are you going to trust to help?

Jonah was in a one-of-a-kind situation. There was no one else to turn to other than God. So that's what he did. He needed that kind of wakeup call, though. Jonah had tried to do things his way instead of God's. But when he found himself living in the middle of a do-as-I-tell-you-or-else situation, it didn't take Jonah long to figure out the "or else" was more than he could handle.

You've done the same thing, haven't you? A bunch of times, I bet. It's ok. We've all been there. It's a lesson despite having countless examples like Jonah we still need to learn for ourselves. You think you can handle something better—that you don't need God's help or that His way isn't always the best or right way. You do that even though...

CASE IN POINT

Jonah thought he had a better way of dealing with the people of Nineveh. Job thought God messed up by allowing Job to be born at all. Peter tried to stop Jesus from going peacefully with the soldiers who came to arrest him.

See? You aren't alone in thinking you know better—that God can't always be trusted to know what's best. But you are wrong. God is the best and most reliable source for help. He gives strength, courage, confidence, and love. He also knows that no matter what ANYONE or ANYTHING else says, YOU ARE VALUABLE. YOUR LIFE MATTERS. YOU ARE NOT WORTHLESS AND YOU HAVE A PURPOSE.

You have probably heard all these things before, but let's take a minute to review...

- You've heard and read the verses in the Bible about being "fearfully and wonderfully made" in Psalm 139.
- You've sat through a bunch of lessons in Genesis 1 on why being made in the image of God should give you the confidence you need to love and respect yourself.
- You've seen skits and had lessons about how and why God gives us all different talents and abilities in 1 Corinthians 12 and that we all have something important to do for God here on Earth.

So, whenever or if you ever start feeling like you are worthless, that your life doesn't matter, that no one loves you, that you don't deserve to live...STOP! Stop feeling and start thinking. Start thinking about the Jesus who died *for you.* Start thinking about the fact that God had your whole life planned for you before you were ever even born. Start thinking about the truth that God doesn't make mistakes, which means you are not a mistake. You have value, purpose, and are of great worth. Stop letting the weight of Satan's lies make you feel defeated and start thinking about what is real—that God's opinion on everything is truth, and His opinion of you is that you are fearfully and wonderfully made!

USE IT FOR YOU

1: How confident are you of your abilities, your value as a person, and qualities you possess that contribute to your family and society? VERY confident, MOSTLY confident, USUALLY confident, SOMETIMES confident, RARELY confident, NEVER confident.

2: Why did you choose the answer you circled in question number one?

3: Who or what makes you think or feel badly about yourself? Why do you allow these people or things to have this effect on you?

4: Have you or someone you know ever thought about or tried to commit suicide?

Here is a prevention hotline resource called *988lifeline.org.* It is completely free.

5: Who can you trust with your thoughts and feelings? Who are the people that have a positive effect on you? Do you spend most of your time around these people? If not, why not?

6: What music, movies, video games, books, television shows, people, social media or other activities do you need to walk away from (and fast!) so that you can do a better job of believing that you are valuable and loved by God—that your life matters a LOT?

MORE FROM THE BIBLE

Look up the following verses. Read each one and think about what it is saying to YOU.

- John 14:27
- Matthew 11:28–30

- John 16:33
- Jeremiah 29:11–12

PRAYER PROMPT

Tell God everything. Tell Him what hurts, scares, bothers, confuses, and makes you angry. Admit your thoughts and feelings to God. He already knows what they are, but He wants to hear you say it and you need to say it to Him. Ask Him to protect you from negative and bad thoughts about yourself and to give you the courage and confidence to be glad and thankful for who He made you to be.

34

WHEN I GROW UP, I WANT TO...

> *Commit your work to the Lord, and your plans will be established.*
>
> — PROVERBS 16:3 ESV

A few chapters back, we talked about how to protect yourself from people who want to put too much pressure on you to make choices and decisions you aren't ready to make or shouldn't be making at all. Now we're going to talk about how to handle the pressure that comes with making important choices and decisions—the ones everyone must make in life.

THE most important decision in this category is the decision to accept Jesus as your Lord and Savior...and then to live out that decision with faithful obedience. After that, the other "biggies" are (not in order of importance) where and if you go to college, your career path, choosing a wife, having a family, where to live, and on and on it goes.

For now, though, we're going to stick with just one: the decision of what you do with your life when it comes to your career. Don't worry, this isn't about trying to tell you what to do or pressuring you to decide on a career path now. This is about giving you some pointers on how to make those decisions when it is time for you to make them.

*God created everyone with a special skill set of abilities and talents. One of the reasons He did that was so that you could work at something you enjoy doing and something you are good at. So, when you start thinking about what you want to do for a career, choose something you enjoy and something you are good at.

*God commanded us and expects us to obey, honor, and respect Him no matter what we are doing, who we are with, or where we go. That means you need to choose a career that won't disrespect God. It also means that no matter what your job is, it needs to be obvious to everyone around you that you are a Christian.

*The *way you do your job* should let people know you are a Christian, too. For example, if you are a coach, you should never treat your team badly. You shouldn't cheat, yell, or cuss at officials, the athletes, or their parents. If you choose a career in marketing or advertising, don't represent products or businesses that promote or candy coat something God has declared to be sinful.

CASE IN POINT

Jacob was a natural born shepherd and herdsman. He had an eye for selecting the best livestock and the ability to feed and care for them to grow to their full potential. Jacob used his skills to raise quality livestock, which in turn made him a wealthy man. He abused his skills by using them to trick and deceive his father-in-law out of good livestock and money.

FYI: There's a lot more to that story. Their family drama is probably where the phrase "dysfunctional family" came from. But that's a lesson in another section.

Saul was a well-educated Jewish man with plenty of self-confidence. He was bold and didn't have any problem standing in front of a crowd to give a speech. He was also the kind of guy who didn't back down from a fight when it came to standing up for what he believed was right.

Those are all good qualities if they are being used to stand up for what is true and right. That's not what Saul was doing, though. He was anti-Jesus and doing everything he could to wipe out Christians and keep them from spreading the message of salvation through Jesus. But God who created Saul with these qualities, decided He wasn't going to allow them to go to waste, so He had Jesus get Saul's attention by a) temporarily blinding him, and b) talking to him from Heaven.

Jesus stopped Saul in his tracks, while Saul was on his way to the city of Damascus to beat up a bunch of Christians and put them in prison. Jesus told Saul he was no longer going to allow him to do that—that it was time Saul put his talents and his gung-ho attitude to work for something important. The Church. Leading people to Jesus. Saul not only listened to what Jesus had to say, but he obeyed. Big time! Saul, whom Jesus renamed Paul, became the most well-known, enthusiastic, dedicated missionary of all time.

USE IT FOR YOU

1: What hobbies and activities do you enjoy most?

2: What are your favorite subjects in school? Which subjects do you make the best grades in?

3: List three jobs/professions you think you would enjoy and do well in?

4: Do you believe you have the patience and would be willing to commit to the training and education it takes to do those jobs? Why or why not?

5: List the three jobs/professions again. Next to each one, write down two or three ways you could share and show your faith and your relationship with Jesus while doing each of them.

MORE FROM THE BIBLE

Look up the following verses. Read each one and think about what it is saying to YOU.

- Proverbs 19:21
- Psalm 37:4
- 1 Timothy 4:8
- Colossians 3:17

PRAYER PROMPT

Thank God for the talents and abilities He has given you and ask Him to guide you in choosing the career He knows is best for you, and to always use your talents to honor Him. Ask God to help you always be a positive example.

35

IT'S UP TO YOU

> *You who are young, be happy while you are young, and let your heart give you joy in the days of your youth. Follow the ways of your heart and whatever your eyes see, but know that for all these things God will bring you into judgment.*
>
> *— ECCLESIASTES 11:9 NIV*

In chapter one you learned (or were reminded) that communicating with God and Jesus starts with prayer, and that you must be the one to initiate the conversation. Now, in this final chapter of the book, you are going to learn (or be reminded) that maintaining that relationship is also up to you. God is always present. Always ready, willing, and able to help, listen, guide, protect, comfort, and all those other things He does so perfectly well. But God never forces Himself on anyone.

Don't worry, though, because even though the choice is yours, once you make that choice you will never ever be alone. Don't let the enemy convince you that you are too young, too busy, too poor, too rich, or too anything else. Daniel was a teenager whose entire nation was taken captive. Joseph was a teenager who was sold into slavery by his own brothers. David was a shepherd boy, who was probably dirty and a bit awkward. Peter, Andrew, James, and John were uneducated, rowdy, hard-working fishermen. Moses was shy, he stuttered, and he was scared to face the people he had run away from. Joshua and Caleb didn't go along with the rest of the group who reported back to Moses that the people in Canaan would be hard to beat.

Do you know what all those guys had in common? They chose to obey.

So, in these final pages of the book we are going to look at some key elements of what it means to *be* a Christian—not do Christianity. Under each one will be a few suggestions on ways you can *be* that kind of person. Then to round things out, there will be a Bible verse for you to read and think about, followed by a few Bible verses for you to look up on your own. Hopefully, by now this book has gotten you in the habit of using the Bible as your guidebook for life and thinking about life in terms of what God wants and expects from you.

Total belief

1. Read the Bible so that you know what it says.
2. Make church and youth group meetings a priority so that you can learn more about the Bible, be encouraged and mentored by more mature Christians, and to form solid friendships with other Christians your age.
3. Ask older Christians (your parents, preacher, youth minister) questions about things you don't understand.
4. Remember that God's opinion on everything is TRUTH. So, if someone tries to make you believe something is true, if it doesn't line up with what the Bible says, it is false.

> *All Scripture is God-breathed and is useful for teaching, rebuking, correcting and training in righteousness, so that the servant of God may be thoroughly equipped for every good work.*
>
> — *2ND TIMOTHY 3:16–17 ESV*

- Proverbs 30:5
- Malachai 3:10
- John 1:1–3

Faith

1. Pray - telling God everything that is on your mind and in your heart. When you tell him what you need and want, He answers.
2. Keep your eyes, ears, heart, and mind open to see and hear God working in your life. Remember that there is no such thing as luck, coincidence, or fate. Everything that happens either comes from God or is allowed by God.
3. Give God a chance to work in your life. Faith only grows and gets stronger when you use it.

> *And without faith it is impossible to please him, for whoever would draw near to God must believe that he exists and that he rewards those who seek him.*
>
> — *HEBREWS 11:6 ESV*

- 2 Corinthians 5:7
- James 2:17
- James 1:6

Faithful Obedience

1. Know what the Bible says and do it. Just do it.
2. Put God first in every situation.
3. We are all going to stand before God someday to be held accountable for the life we have lived and to be judged. Use this TRUTH to direct your decision-making and your actions.

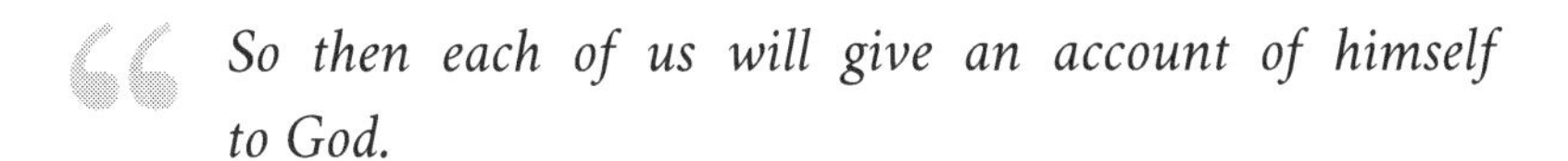

> *So then each of us will give an account of himself to God.*
>
> — *ROMANS 14:12 ESV*

- Matthew 12:36–37
- Jeremiah 17:10
- John 14:23
- Ecclesiastes 12:13

Love

1. Love God first by always putting Him first.
2. Live a grateful life because of the enormous gift of life and salvation through Jesus that God has given you.
3. Treat others the way you want them to treat you.
4. Learn to filter your actions and your words through the definition God gives us of love (1 Corinthians 13:4–7)

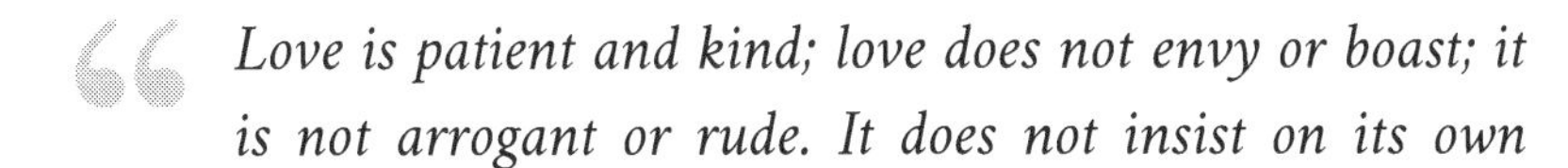

> *Love is patient and kind; love does not envy or boast; it is not arrogant or rude. It does not insist on its own*

> *way; it is not irritable or resentful; it does not rejoice at wrongdoing, but rejoices with the truth. Love bears all things, believes all things, hopes all things, endures all things. Love never ends.*
>
> — 1ST CORINTHIANS 13:4–7 ESV

- 1 Corinthians 16:14
- Colossians 3:14
- Mark 12:29–31

Joy and Contentment

1. Understand that joy and contentment are NOT feelings. Joy and contentment are what you choose to be your mindset (attitude, belief, conviction) no matter what is going on around you. In other words, your attitude isn't all wishy-washy depending on what is going on around you. You choose to remember that *the joy of the Lord is your strength,* and that you will *be content in all circumstances* because you know God will never allow you to face more than the two of you can handle together, and that He will always bring something good out of a situation if you trust Him to do so.
2. Do your best to stay away from negative people and other negative influences (books, television, music, t-shirts, video games).
3. Choose to serve others by volunteering in your church, your community, and your home.

4. Be grateful and thankful. Tell your parents thank you for letting you participate in extracurricular activities and taking the time to cheer you on. Thank your mom when she fixes your favorite foods and for doing your laundry. Tell your dad thank you for taking the time to throw or kick the ball around. Say thanks to the lunch lady when you get your lunch tray. Say thanks to the school counselor for helping you with college applications. Say thanks to your youth minister for all he or she does. Say thanks to people who hold a door open, and the teacher who helps you with that pesky math homework.

Consider it pure joy, my brothers and sisters, whenever you face trials of many kinds, because you know that the testing of your faith produces perseverance.

— *JAMES 1:2–3 NIV*

- Proverbs 17:22
- Romans 12:12
- Psalm 118:24
- 1 Peter 1:8–9

Kindness and Compassion

1. Be nice. Treat people the way you want to be treated.
2. Look around. Who needs your help? Who can you share with? Where can you volunteer your time and talents?
3. Compliment people. I know for guys that can be a little awkward, but you don't have to be mushy. Simple, sincere comments like, "Great job!" "Way to go!" "Impressive!" and "You make it look so easy" are compliments that make anyone feel good about themselves.
4. Use your manners. Notice who is sitting alone in the lunchroom and go sit by them. Step up and stand by the kids being bullied. Be friendly to the kids who seem to have no friends. Don't ever make fun of someone.

> *But if anyone has the world's goods and sees his brother in need, yet closes his heart against him, how does God's love abide in him?*
>
> — *1 JOHN 3:17 ESV*

- Galatians 6:10
- Acts 20:35
- Proverbs 21:21

Forgiveness

1. Let it go! Whatever "it" is, let it go. Remember that forgiveness is about giving you a clean heart and mind and a clear conscience.
2. Remember that God will not forgive your sins if you don't forgive people who hurt and offend you.
3. You and you alone have the power to choose how you respond and react to what happens to you. Use this power wisely.
4. Whenever you are tempted to be *un*forgiving, remember that God always forgives you when you ask Him to.

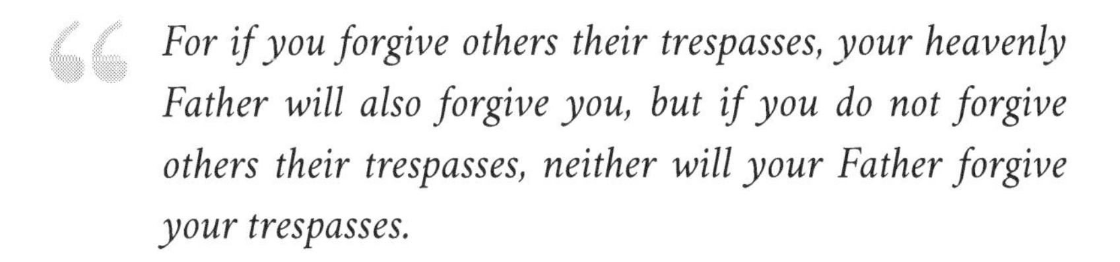

For if you forgive others their trespasses, your heavenly Father will also forgive you, but if you do not forgive others their trespasses, neither will your Father forgive your trespasses.

— *MATTHEW 6:14–15 ESV*

- Matthew 18:21–22
- Psalm 103–10–14
- Acts 2:38
- Proverbs 28:13

Humility

1. The best definition or explanation of humility I have ever seen is this: Humility isn't thinking you are less of a person than others. Humility is thinking about yourself less than you think of others. Read that two or three times until it sticks.
2. What are you good at? Use these talents to help others.
3. Do an anonymous random act of kindness once or twice a week.
4. When someone compliments you, smile and say thank you. Don't be ashamed or embarrassed to be recognized and appreciated for what you do. Just be sure to thank God for your abilities and make sure you don't misuse or abuse them.

> *Humble yourselves before the Lord, and he will exalt you.*
>
> — *JAMES 4:10 ESV*

- 1 Peter 5:5
- Micah 6:8
- Philippians 2:3

PRAYER PROMPT

Ask God to keep you focused on learning and growing to be more and more like Him. Tell God which areas you struggle with and ask Him to give you the courage to not give up.

AUTHOR'S NOTE

My Dear Reader,

First of all, I want to express my deepest gratitude for taking the time to read this devotional. It's an honor to be able to share my thoughts and insights with you. I hope that you found them valuable and meaningful, and it was a game changer for you.

As a teenager, you are in a unique position to develop your leadership skills, build your confidence, and grow your faith. These are all crucial aspects of becoming the person you want to be, and I'm so glad that you are investing in yourself in this way.

I hope the devotions in this book have given you some practical tools and strategies for achieving your goals and overcoming challenges. I also hope that they have inspired you to take bold action and pursue your passions with confidence and enthusiasm.

Remember, leadership is not just about being in charge; it's about serving others and making a positive difference in the world. Confidence is not just about feeling good about yourself; it's about recognizing your strengths and using them to achieve your goals. Your faith is not just about believing in God; it's about living out your beliefs in every aspect of your life.

As you continue your journey of personal growth and development, I encourage you to keep these principles in mind. Always strive to be a servant leader, to believe in yourself, and to live out your faith in a way that inspires others.

Continue to build upon this firm foundation in Christ that you have set in place and allow God to light your path by always putting Him first. Express daily gratitude for the life you have been given and always see the good in every situation. If you do this, nothing in this world will be able to keep you down. There is no storm, no valley, or shadow that is more powerful than the name of Jesus.

Thank you again for reading this devotional. I pray that you live an adventurous, healthy life full of joy and love. For additional resources, including a devotional worksheet designed to help you feel a closer connection with God by identifying and eliminating any spiritual blockages you may have, please visit ***olivebranchpublishing.com***.

Please scan the QR code below to leave a quick review describing your experience with this devotional.

There is a young man out there struggling and your review has the potential to completely change his life. Let's make a difference together!

Sincerely,
Hillary Olive

Printed in Great Britain
by Amazon